44 Ways to Increase Church Attendance

44 WAYS TO INCREASE CHURCH ATTENDANCE

Lyle E. Schaller

Illustrated by Edward Lee Tucker

ABINGDON PRESS
NASHVILLE

44 WAYS TO INCREASE CHURCH ATTENDANCE

Library of Congress Cataloging-in-Publication Data

Schaller, Lyle E.
44 ways to increase church attendance.
1. Church attendance. I. Title. II. Title:
Forty-four ways to increase church attendance.
BV652.5.S29   1988   254'.5   87-15281

ISBN 0-687-13287-8
(alk. paper)

MANUFACTURED BY THE PARTHENON PRESS AT
NASHVILLE, TENNESSEE, UNITED STATES OF AMERICA

To
Agnes
and
Donna Loraine

CONTENTS

INTRODUCTION

W hy should we be interested in increasing our worship attendance?" demanded a member of the Maple Grove Church. "We're averaging about 145 at Sunday morning worship. We've been on that plateau for several years, that's about all our building will accommodate unless we go to two services, and nobody here wants to do that, or unless we enlarge the building, and that would cost a lot of money. Why don't you leave us alone?"

"Yeah, instead of talking about our church growing in numbers, why don't you start more new churches?" added a supporting voice. "We're just a good comfortable size as we are now. We have a wonderful fellowship and we're the right size to enable everyone to know everyone else. Everyone knows size produces anonymity. Why do you want to disturb us with all these ways that might increase our church attendance? Why should we try to become a bigger church and have to deal with all the problems confronting those big churches when we like it the way it is here? We're small enough for everyone to know everyone else, but big enough to offer a full-scale program."

While rarely stated that bluntly, these statements represent the perspective of a very large number of church leaders who are satisfied with the status quo.

Considerable evidence can be mustered to support their position. From a member point of view the congregation averaging seventy-five to eighty-five at worship on Sunday morning may be the most comfortable-sized church in American Protestantism. It is small enough for members to know and care for one another. It is sufficiently large to offer a meaningful worship experience, to include a chancel choir and to maintain a good Sunday school. It is small enough that the time frame for planning can be comfortably short, the internal communication system can be largely informal, inexpensive, and effective. The two limitations often are (a) difficulty in providing the financial support necessary for a long-term pastorate and (b) difficulty in building and maintaining a meeting place. Many small congregations, however, have overcome these by (a) finding a pastor who has a spouse with full-time employment who is reluctant to change jobs and (b) relying on the contributions of past generations to purchase the land and construct the building.

Perhaps the second most comfortable-sized congregation is the one averaging 135 to 160 at worship on Sunday morning. It enjoys the benefits of being relatively small (although in fact it is larger than four out of five Protestant congregations on the North American continent), but usually possesses all the resources necessary for a full-scale program.

This size congregation normally can offer, if it so chooses and if the building grants permission, two *different* worship experiences on Sunday morning to meet two different sets of needs. It usually can offer a full-scale ministry of Christian education, an attractive youth program, two or three or four choirs, a women's organization with three or four circles, some specialized classes and possibly a men's fellowship. It normally includes sufficient people to staff all the positions for volunteers, to challenge the skills and energy of a full-time pastor and to maintain an attractive meeting place. That size congregation usually is able to allocate at least 15 percent of all contributions to outreach, to attract enough new members to replace the 5 or 6 percent who disappear every year, to provide the pastor with at least twenty-five or thirty hours of secretarial help every week, and to pay all the bills without making money the top agenda item at every meeting of the governing board. In many respects it is an optimum-sized congregation.

The argument for the status quo can be reinforced by the fact that larger congregations do have problems rarely faced by smaller churches. These include anonymity, the need to create and maintain an expensive and redundant internal communication system; the necessity of a cooperative staff team; a higher level of per-member giving simply to be able to pay all the bills; a more complicated schedule; a much higher rate of turnover in the membership (often approaching 12 to 15 percent annually in the very large and rapidly growing churches); a turnover in the staff that means community building among the staff is rarely completed; maintaining a more expensive meeting place; responding to the expectations outsiders place on the large church; a greater need for off-street parking; the expectations by the members for high quality whether one refers to the preaching, the music, the rest rooms or the youth program; and the pressures from the 3 to 5 percent of the members who are not satisfied with the status quo. (Three percent in a hundred-member church represents three individuals, and they often can be won over by the charm of the pastor. Three percent in a thousand-member church can mean a cohesive and

powerful group of thirty people determined to replace the current senior minister.)

The most persuasive argument against reading this book can be summarized in eight terrifying words. *What if we try it and it works?* If a congregation tries a new approach to ministry and it fails, little harm is done. Usually everything soon returns to the way it was before, and life goes on. The great risk is to implement a new idea that may work. If it does, the world will never be the same again!

Every one of the forty-four suggestions in this book on increasing the Sunday morning church attendance has been tried in scores of congregations. Every one can work. Some have produced the desired results in four out of five congregations. Others consistently have produced results that exceeded expectations. A few require a long time period before results are visible. Several do require a combination of factors to work.

When all is said and done, however, there are only two, not forty-four, ways to increase attendance in any congregation. One is to increase the frequency of attendance of those who are now attending. A not uncommon pattern today is when an attendance survey is conducted over four consecutive Sundays, one-fifth of the members will be present on every Sunday, 30 percent will attend on two or three out of those four Sundays, 20 percent will attend once and 30 percent will be absent on all four Sundays. If one-half of those who missed all four Sundays can be persuaded to attend at least once or twice a month, and if those who were present only once out of four Sundays begin to attend two or three times a

month, the average attendance will rise dramatically. (See the first suggestion in chapter 6.)

The second approach is to reach more people. If instead of two hundred different people attending at least once during a month's time, that number can be increased to three hundred (some of whom may be formerly inactive members) and if the frequency of attendance of the original two hundred does not decrease, the average attendance will climb significantly.

Many of the suggestions in this book are designed to increase the frequency of attendance. Others are designed to attract first-time visitors and a few are included to increase the probability that first-time visitors will return the following Sunday. The purposes of the suggestions are varied and several are mutually reinforcing.

The critical point, however, is these are tested ideas

that have worked and the reader should be warned that few things in this world have the power of a new idea.

In simple terms this book has not been written for those who are comfortable with the status quo. This book has been written for leaders in local churches who share six convictions.

First, they are convinced of the power of God's Word and they are convinced that when people hear God's Word preached, lives are changed.

Second, they are convinced that by definition Christians are called to come together to worship God and to share in the sacraments or ordinances of the church.

Third, they take literally and seriously the Great Commission (Matt. 28:19-20) and feel compelled by the power of those words to follow that directive.

Fourth, they believe

that every worshiping community should be actively engaged in confronting more and more people with the Good News that Jesus Christ is Lord and Savior and that their own local church is not exempt from that imperative.

Fifth, they are venturesome, risk-taking persons who are willing, if not eager, to make the changes necessary to bring more people into that worshiping community of which they are members.

Sixth, they are willing to accept the role of agents of intentional change from within an organization (see chapter 7) and understand that it always brings unanticipated consequences, discontinuity, and other threats to the status quo. *Jake Flak*

The forty-four suggestions for increasing the attendance at corporate worship are divided among six chapters. The first twelve are directed at the Sunday morning worship experience and increasing its attractiveness. The next five overlap the first somewhat, but are focused on the Sunday morning schedule.

While this is rarely discussed in these terms, every congregation with no exceptions has developed a series of operational policies that influence church attendance. Seven of these are reviewed in the third chapter. For some congregations this may be the appropriate beginning point in any effort to increase church attendance.

Once upon a time pastoral calling was the most productive and cost-effective means of increasing attendance. Today, in a growing proportion of congregations, program is far more influential both in influencing the frequency of attendance of members and in attracting new members. Five suggestions on strengthening program as a means of increasing church attendance are discussed in the fourth chapter.

While frequently overlooked, real estate considerations often are remarkably influential in church attendance and eleven of these are reviewed in the fifth chapter.

From a long-term comprehensive point of view many congregations would be well advised to look at institutional factors if they are serious about increasing the size of the crowd on Sunday morning. Four of these are reviewed in the sixth chapter.

Finally, for many readers the critical question concerns the implementation of some of these suggestions. Often that turns out to be a more complex issue than simply increasing the size of the crowd. It really is a process of planned change. That is the subject of the final chapter.

Cartoons often can be very useful in communicating new ideas to people, so scattered throughout this volume is a series of cartoons in which Friar Tuck speaks to the subject under discussion. Individuals purchasing this book are hereby granted permission to reproduce these cartoons in local church publications or in presentations at congregational gatherings. Permission is specifically withheld for reproducing these cartoons, or any other parts of this book, in motion picture films, video tapes, slides, books, magazines, denominational publications, or in any other form or manner.

- most churches end up on a plateau
- hard to move out of that
there will be leaders
- churches that grow will pay attention
to needs & build program around
- most "missionary" church can be
is to meet needs by program,
rather than visitation by pastor.

1   *BEGIN WITH THE WORSHIP EXPERIENCE*

Some congregations carefully and regularly record the attendance at Sunday morning worship; others place a greater emphasis on the number of people attending Sunday school while many congregations keep a record of both.

WHO AND WHAT FOLKS COME FOR ARE BIG REASONS WHY THEY STAY!

A Sense of Belonging and Friends

—FRIAR TUCK

When asked why they return Sunday after Sunday, the respondents to scores of surveys have given the same basic answer, "I had such a good experience last Sunday I wanted to come back." Those questioned about worship attendance usually lift up one or both of two factors. First, this was a meaningful worship experience which spoke to that person in terms of that individual's religious needs.

For many, a close second is that Sunday morning is not only a time for the corporate worship of God, but also an opportunity to share concerns, joys, and fellowship with other Christians who together constitute a loving, supportive, hopeful, caring, forgiving, and sustaining covenant community. This second attraction often is more obvious and more widely shared in smaller congregations than in large ones where only a handful of people can call every other member by name. For many people this is the unique characteristic of the small church and its distinctive reason for being.

The natural tendency, however, is for this fellowship to be inwardly focused on this circle of long-time friends. One result is the first-time visitor may feel like an outsider and leave firmly convinced this is a member-oriented congregation not interested in strangers.

The larger the number of people present on Sunday morning, the more likely this will happen. The members claim, "This is a friendly church!" but the outsider may interpret that to mean the insiders are friendly with one another. The larger the number of people present on Sunday morning, the more likely that a significant number of members also will feel like outsiders and depart knowing that if they fail to return next Sunday, no one will miss them. That helps explain why the worship-attendance-to-membership ratio often declines as membership increases.

For those interested in church growth the obvious conclusion is the larger the size of the congregation, the more likely the quality and depth of meaning of the worship experience will be the primary reason why first-time visitors return. The smaller the congregation, the more likely the inclusionary or exclusionary character of the fellowship will be the number-one factor in determining whether first-time visitors return.

For those interested in increasing the number of people present for corporate worship these two factors offer a useful context for looking at a dozen ways to increase attendance. Let us begin by looking at the worship experience itself as a way to increase attendance.

For the past fifteen years or more the conventional wisdom has declared it is the churches that offer a fundamentalist version of the Christian faith that are growing. Likewise the widely accepted stereotype is that all those huge congregations are theologically conservative.

First-hand visits to dozens of these churches and interviews with adults who recently joined them suggest this is a misleading oversimplification. Those who are not comfortable with theologically conservative interpretations of the Scriptures should be careful not to accept that single factor analysis of contemporary reality. Life is far too complicated for such simple analysis. This can be illustrated by these suggestions on how to increase attendance in your church.

1. Offer a Note of Hope

Perhaps the most common characteristic of the churches that are attracting increasing numbers of people today is not where the minister is on the theological spectrum or the denominational affiliation, but on what people hear and feel during the worship experience. This is a note of hope.

When asked what he preached, one Presbyterian minister who has seen his attendance quadruple in fourteen years replied, "I try to help my people get from Sunday morning to at least Friday. I offer them a note of help. I keep telling them God created this world and He is still at work in His world. If He hasn't given up on us, we should be able to have faith in Him."

In very simple terms the most important single factor in increasing worship attendance is to present the Good

News as good news. The idea that the Christian faith offers hope and attracts people who have hope was a dominant characteristic of the New Testament churches.[1]

The one theme that is common to churches that are attracting more people is the theme of hope. This may be expressed as "our team is winning," which was a highly visible part of frontier Methodism,[2] or it may be expressed simply as "God loves you and we love you," but that note of hope and optimism about the future is a powerful factor in determining the size of the crowd. A Presbyterian congregation on the north side of Omaha, for example, has created its own colorful bulletin covers designed to convey a sense of joy, hope, and God's love for His children as a part of a larger effort to offer a note of hope.

The negative side of that same point has been illustrated repeatedly in the self-fulfilling prophecies expressed in those Anglo inner-city congregations founded in the nineteenth century or in that small rural church when nearly every Sunday brought a reaffirmation of the message, "Within a few years this church will close."

---

[1]Wayne A. Meeks, *The First Urban Christians* (New Haven: Yale University Press, 1982).

[2]When the nineteenth-century agnostic Robert G. Ingersoll declared, "The churches are dying out all over the land . . . ," Chaplain Charles C. McCabe, assistant secretary of the Church Extension Society of The Methodist Episcopal Church, replied with a famous telegram. "Dear Robert: 'All hail the power of Jesus' name'—we are building more than one Methodist Church for every day in the year, and propose to make it two a day!" (Signed) C. C. McCabe. Quoted in Halford E. Luccock et al., *The Story of Methodism* (Nashville: Abingdon Press, 1949), p. 447.

Contemporary examples of the appeal of being part of a "winning team" are that attendance usually increases during the concluding months of a major building program, or with the arrival of the new minister following a disastrous pastorate, or when a congregation completes a challenging mission goal or, most important of all, on Easter Sunday.

Throughout human history people have flocked to hear those who have brought a note of hope and been repelled by those who sought to build a following on a note of despair. How that word of hope is expressed will vary from preacher to preacher and from congregation to congregation, but that is the first question to examine for those who are interested in increasing the level of church attendance.

Make your pastor a better preacher or die of boredom trying! —FRIAR TUCK

2. *Enhance the Quality of Preaching*

A second part of a larger strategy to increase church attendance may be to improve the quality of preaching. The last two decades of the twentieth century have brought a renewed recognition of the value of biblical preaching.

This can take several forms. One is the traditional expository preaching. A second is the resurgence of interest in storytelling as the preacher retells the biblical narrative in contemporary language and imagery. A third is the teaching sermon.

Many pastors concerned with the issue of the relevance of preaching have created ad hoc sermon preparation committees. One form is to bring together

SIX OR SEVEN WEEKS TOGETHER PRODUCES A BONDING EFFECT!

Sermon Preparation Groups

—FRIAR TUCK

a half dozen laypersons who represent three or four generations and ask them to meet for one evening a week for four to six weeks. The first evening is spent studying the text the minister has chosen for a future sermon and the biblical context for that passage. The second and third evenings are devoted to a discussion of how that passage of Scripture speaks to each member of that group. The fourth and fifth evenings are spent preparing an outline for a sermon based on that text. (The reason for two evenings on each phase of the process is that it allows people to return a week later and incorporate their second thoughts into the discussion. Most normal people do their best thinking on the way home from the meeting.) The sixth and perhaps a seventh evening enable the laypersons to critique the outline and a preliminary draft of the proposed sermon.[3]

Scores of ministers report that following this procedure four times a year with four different groups of members not only has a positive impact on the relevance of the sermon and on worship attendance, but also produces several important fringe benefits. One is the participants

---

[3]An exceptionally lucid and useful essay on how to become a better preacher is Fred E. Luchs, "You Can Be a Better Preacher," *Monday Morning,* February 20, 1984, pp. 15-16.

become closer to one another after six or seven weeks together in a shared experience. A second is new opportunities for more meaningful pastoral care. A third is an increase in the number of volunteers. A fourth is the spontaneous emergence of new support groups for the pastor. A fifth is some of the members of these groups report that experience has had a profound impact on their own religious pilgrimage. It must be recognized, however, that this experience will not be compatible with the personality and priorities of every minister.

Another approach to improving the quality of the preaching and particularly the delivery is now more widely available than formerly. This is the home video camera. While it requires considerable courage and a strong desire for self-improvement, watching oneself delivering a sermon on video tape can be both a humbling and an enlightening experience.

A somewhat less threatening road to self-improvement is followed by those ministers who, on three or four occasions a year, ask for five or six volunteers to constitute a sermon evaluation committee. A typical format brings these lay volunteers together first for two evenings during which they formulate and discuss the appropriate criteria for the evaluation of a sermon. Pastors have varying degrees of involvement in that process. After two such sessions these folks come to the Sunday morning worship experience and, obviously, listen carefully to the sermon. A couple of evenings later they meet with the preacher to share their reflections and insights. In at least a few cases the group worships with another congregation first before the formal evaluation of their own minister's sermon.

Woe unto those
who cannot stay awake
during their own
sermon, video-reruns!
—FRIAR TUCK

This "practice run" enhances their self-confidence, broadens their comparison base and may suggest additional criteria. (It should be noted that every pastor's preaching is evaluated by laypersons every week. This particular process provides more intentionality about the criteria and improves the accuracy of the feedback.)

A less threatening and far more widely used approach is the "talk back" session following worship. Sometimes this takes the form of an ongoing adult class that the preacher meets with following worship; more often it is more of an ad hoc gathering. Frequently the focus of the discussion is on the content, but, if the minister is willing, the focus can be shifted to delivery and to eliciting suggestions on improving content and/or delivery.

Many of the best preachers also are willing to subject themselves to the discipline of preparing a series of sermons on a specific subject. A very common example is the Ten Commandments. Another is a series on temptations. A third is on the saints of the faith. A fourth is on basic doctrines.

A thoughtfully planned and carefully prepared series of sermons often can produce both better preaching and an increase in worship attendance.

3. Schedule More Preachers

For those congregations that have two or more good preachers available, one of the most effective means of increasing the attendance at Sunday morning worship is to schedule two different preachers for thirty-five or more Sundays a year.

The basic assumption on which this alternative is based is the fact that it is increasingly rare when one person can deliver a sermon that is equally meaningful to everyone in the room. Those present come with different agendas, some at a different stage in their faith journey than others. Many have not been to seminary and thus have not been taught the characteristics of an excellent sermon and at least a few simply do not find that minister to be on their religious wave length.

An increasingly common response to the growing diversity of the religious needs of the people is to schedule one minister to preach at the first service and another at the second hour. In literally dozens of churches the associate minister preaches at the first hour on thirty-five Sundays a year while the senior pastor preaches at the other service, or sometimes at the other two services.

The most widespread objection to this concept is, "How can you justify the investment in time for an extra sermon preparation for only sixty to a hundred people?"

At least a half dozen factors should be discussed when that objective is raised. The most obvious is that every week at least 150,000 Protestant ministers prepare a sermon that will be heard by no more than one hundred persons and frequently fewer than sixty. Is that objection suggesting that every small church should be closed?

More important is the issue of values and goals.
Which is the more important? The most efficient use of
ministerial time and energy? Or to bring together a
larger number of people to hear the Word? Or to
increase the number of people who leave grateful they
came that day?

Some will object, "Maybe that would work in a big
congregation, but our church is too small to try anything
like that." That comment misses the key point. The
number-one issue in considering this alternative is not
size, but rather the theological diversity of the membership. The more homogeneous the membership, the less
likely this will be a wise course of action. The more
heterogeneous the membership, the greater the possibility that it will result in an increase in attendance. As a
general rule the most homogeneous congregations are
those in which the vast majority of the present members
have joined since the arrival of the present pastor. The
most heterogeneous are those in which (a) at least
one-half of today's members joined before the arrival of
the past two ministers and/or (b) a substantial proportion
of today's members married into this congregation and/or
(c) at least one-fourth of today's members were born in
the 1930–45 era and at least another fourth were born
after 1956 and/or (d) the Sunday morning worship
attendance-to-membership ratio is under 60 percent.

The fourth factor that should be discussed, and one that
often is voiced as a potential objection, is the availability of
a second preacher for that many Sundays. Alternatives
include retired ministers, a pre-theological student at a
nearby college, a lay preacher, a chaplain in a nearby
institution, a seminary graduate now employed in a
secular job, a seminary or college teacher, one-half of that

clergy couple serving another congregation within thirty or forty miles, a seminary student, a retired military chaplain, or the associate minister or a retired missionary.

A fifth issue that is almost certain to be raised in those churches with only one minister on the payroll is cost. How can we afford it? First of all, can you afford not to do it if it will increase your worship attendance? Second, in most churches the total amount of member giving is directly related to the number of people at worship on Sunday morning. The congregation averaging 180 at worship typically receives more than twice as many dollars annually from member giving as the church averaging a hundred at worship. While a 20 percent increase in worship attendance may not immediately result in a 20 percent increase in contributions, the two often go together. In the vast majority of congregations Sunday morning worship is the only activity or program that pays its way.

Finally, some will object this will promote a rivalry between the two preachers and members will identify a "winner" and a "loser" in terms of the size of the crowd. Experience does not support that fear. The people who attend one service tend to be oblivious about what is happening at the other hour. They come to have their religious needs met, not to make comparisons. They do not have the experience on which to make those kinds of comparisons. This approach does require, however, two preachers who are both personally and professionally secure, who differ in preaching styles and theology and who complement rather than duplicate one another.

Why does this increase attendance? The most obvious reason is it increases the chances of meeting the religious needs of a larger number of people. It also can offer the choice of worship followed by Sunday school for those who prefer that schedule and Sunday school followed by worship for those who prefer that schedule. Typically each minister will preach at both services about six or eight times a year; thus everyone has the chance to listen to the other preacher. It also can result in doubling the number of laypersons who are actively involved as members of a choir, as ushers, as liturgists, or as greeters.

The two big surprises it often produces are (a) a few people will attend both services on many Sundays and (b) with some couples the wife will attend at one hour and the husband at the other hour. There is no law against either practice and both are more attractive than the more common alternative of the husband remaining at home while the wife goes to church.

4. Hasten the Pace

One of the most common reasons given by church members when asked why they attend worship only infrequently is, "It's boring." Unfortunately that often may be an accurate diagnosis. Too often the service is slow paced, dull, repetitive, filled with long pauses and without frequent changes of pace.

A direct action response is to accelerate the pace. This can be achieved by reducing the repetition, by including several musical responses (the larger the congregation, the greater the need for a faster pace and the more likely the musical resources will be available), by cutting out many of the excessively long pauses, by reducing the length of the sermon to fifteen to twenty minutes or less and including two or three or four briefer prayers rather than one long prayer. If oral announcements must be made about parish life, and a very good case can be made for including them, they should be no longer than fifty to sixty seconds total. If more time is required, it can help to have two different individuals share in making the announcements. The most effective means of creating the impression of a faster pace is to begin exactly on time and conclude one or two minutes *before* the announced time.

This issue of pace is an especially significant factor (a) when the number of people gathered for corporate worship exceeds eighty-five or ninety (60 percent of all Protestant congregations average fewer than a hundred at worship) and (b) when at least two-thirds of the people in the room are under forty-five years of age and are accustomed to the faster pace taught them by television.

A persuasive argument can be made that the most significant single influence of television on the churches has been to teach people to expect a fast-paced presentation.

5. Place Greater Weight on Intercessory Prayer

The past two decades clearly have brought a renewed interest in intercessory prayer. Why this has happened obviously is speculation. From the perspective of the year A.D. 2029, church historians may be referring to the rediscovery of the Holy Spirit as the dominant Christian trend of the last third of the twentieth century. That may be one factor behind this trend. A second may be the rediscovery, especially

Intercessory Prayer

...a great way of getting ourselves off our hands!

—FRIAR TUCK

by many scientifically trained adults, that we are really dependent on God, not on ourselves. A third is the current search for transcendence. A fourth factor may be the resurgence of interest in the healing ministry of Christ and the emergence of several movements built around that ministry. A fifth reason behind this trend may be the general shift toward a theologically more conservative stance by many pastors, especially those who entered the ministry since 1975. Whatever the reasons, it appears more churches are lifting up the importance of intercessory prayer.

One of the more widely followed procedures is for the pastor to come out of the chancel and walk among the people while asking them to lift up their jobs and concerns. These are then incorporated into the pastoral prayer.

One congregation has placed a large cork bulletin board on the wall in the narthex between the two sets of doors leading into the nave. Persons coming to worship are invited to thumb tack their written prayer requests to that bulletin board before entering to worship. During the first hymn an usher collects these and brings them in to the minister who includes them in the pastoral prayer.

Hundreds of congregations place printed PRAYER REQUEST cards in the pew racks. Worshipers are invited to fill out one of these cards before the service begins, and the ushers collect them. Later the pastor incorporates these into the pastoral prayer.

One pastor frequently prefaces the pastoral prayer with the statement, "Today the pastoral prayer is divided into three parts; first, a prayer of thanksgiving; second, a prayer of intercession; and third, a prayer of petition. At the end of each of these parts each member of the congregation is asked to respond with an 'Amen!' In that way the prayer of the pastor becomes the prayer of the people, not just of the minister."

Several larger congregations that mail the bulletin to members early in the week duplicate a list of the prayer concerns late Saturday so as to include the most recent births, hospitalizations, accidents, and joys. That list is inserted in the bulletins before they are distributed on Sunday morning.

In many other congregations the explicit encouragement of intercessory prayer is not limited to the formal worship services, but is expressed through the creation of prayer groups or prayer chains that are actively involved in intercessory prayer throughout the week. If someone is about to undergo surgery, for example, this fact is made known to one or more of the prayer groups, and intercessory prayer is offered up to God, before, during, and after the surgery. Or someone may call the member of the prayer chain who is responsible for receiving prayer requests on that day or that week. After the call has been received, that person calls the other members of the prayer chain to ask them individually to share in this prayer of intercession.

While it is impossible to prove cause and effect, the evidence strongly suggests that those churches that

...AND WHERE IT LANDS WE REALLY DO CARE!

If we keep in touch
chances are
we'll never lose them!

FRIAR TUCK

place a highly visible emphasis on the power of intercessory prayer have a higher ratio of worship attendance to membership than those that give it low visibility.

6. Use the Mails

An increasingly common practice among ministers is to mail every member a personal handwritten note on special occasions such as a birthday, the first day of first grade, a wedding anniversary, a promotion at work, graduation, the birth of a grandchild, or the completion of a special task in the church.

Perhaps the four most powerful letters a minister can mail are (a) the note to the widow on the anniversary of her husband's death, (b) the note to be waiting when the first grader comes home after that first day in school, (c) the letter to the baby who was baptized on the previous Sunday, and (d) a note of thanks to a volunteer. A reasonable goal is every member will receive four to seven notes every year from the pastor (or in larger congregations from a member of the staff).

Among the reasons why this is a growing practice are these six.

First, nearly every minister recognizes that an important component of pastoral care is the affirming of the distinctive personality and concerns of each member. A note written to arrive on a wedding anniversary or a birthday or other special day is the easiest and most economical method of offering this affirmation. (*Note:* Some pastors prefer to do this via a telephone call rather than a personal note.)

Second, nearly every minister spends some time out of town at conferences, on vacation, in continuing education events, and on denominational committees. By planning ahead and writing the personal notes in advance, one very important dimension of pastoral care is not interrupted by these trips out of town. The member receives the message of remembrance or gratitude on the special day, not on the day the letter is written!

Third, a remarkably large number of individuals, including both six-year-olds and seventy-six-year-olds, save, treasure, and reread these personal notes from "my minister." It is much more difficult to save, treasure, and rehear a telephone message or a greeting received on the way out of the worship service.

Fourth, many ministers have discovered they can write two dozen notes in much less time than is required to complete *ten* telephone calls or to make five home visits. One person unilaterally can complete the task of writing and mailing a brief handwritten note, but the cooperation and active participation of the respondent is required to complete a telephone call or to complete a home visit. In other words, this procedure can eliminate that list of telephone calls or visits that did not get made and thus cause the pastor to end the day with a feeling of accomplishment rather than with a sense of disappointment and frustration. This is especially important in those congregations that include many two-career couples.

Fifth, the recognition of special days in the lives of members is one means of offsetting the discontinuity that is an inevitable by-product of a change of ministers. When the newly arrived minister mails twenty to a hundred notes every week, beginning with that very first week, that is a quick and effective way to be perceived as "my pastor" by a growing number of people.

Finally, when a person receives a note from the pastor during the week, it increases the chances of that member being at worship the following Sunday morning.

7. Call on the People

While it is an expensive course of action in terms of time, energy, and frustration when people are not at home, the most effective single approach to increasing church attendance in perhaps seven out of ten of all Protestant churches is for the minister to call in every home at least twice a year. In the 1950s that would have been at the top of this list. Today it is far more difficult to find people at home at an hour convenient to everyone, and the members of many congregations today often are scattered over two or three times as many square miles so it is a far more costly effort.

The cynics may contend that the results of this is that the members "return the call" the following Sunday, but it does work.

8. Involve More People

A less expensive, but perhaps more complex, approach is to involve more people in an active role in the Sunday morning worship experience. One approach is to include one or more carefully trained lay liturgists in conducting the service. (*Caution:* The training is important. If the lay liturgist cannot be heard or understood, that may decrease the attendance next week!) Another is to include two or three or four or five different musical groups each week. A third is to use ushers inside the building and to organize a corps of trained people to greet people *outside* the building and to accompany first-time visitors into the building. (This is very important for those congregations seeking to increase the proportion of first-time visitors who return the following Sunday.) A fourth is creation of a liturgical dance group. A fifth is the special recognition event such as presenting a Bible to each third-grader or the dedication of the Sunday school teachers on one Sunday or a thank-you service for persons completing a term in office.

ON THIS SPECIAL
GROUND HOG SUNDAY
WE EAGERLY AWAIT
THE ADVENT OF SPRING

Special
Sundays
—FRIAR TUCK

9. Schedule More Special Sundays

While this must be adapted to be compatible with the values, personality, and goals of your congregation (and with the values, personality, and goals of the pastor), one of the most effective means of increasing church attendance is to schedule twenty to forty special Sundays every year.

The possibilities are limited only by the imaginations of those doing the planning. A few examples will illustrate what might be done. One set of special Sundays involves the recognition of those in a special vocation or occupation such as health care or the local volunteer fire department or law enforcement or public education or Scouting.

The obvious group of special Sundays includes the first Sunday of Lent, Palm Sunday, Easter, Pentecost, World Communion, All Saints Day, Advent, and Christmas.

Others include the mid-January commemoration of the birthday of Martin Luther King, Jr., Veterans Sunday, Independence Sunday, Father's Day, Brotherhood Sunday, Missionary Sunday, Mother's Day, World Hunger Sunday, One Great Hour of Sharing, Laity Sunday, the Sunday before Thanksgiving Day,

World Peace Sunday, and Labor Sunday.

A fourth group of special days could include the annual weekend celebration of the anniversary of the founding of this congregation, the Sunday in mid-February that celebrates marriages, the Sunday honoring the anniversary of the ordination (or installation) of our current pastor, the installation

service for the new members of the governing board and/or for the new officers of the women's organization, and the Sunday in which special membership pins are presented to each person who has been a member of this congregation for at least twenty-five years.

Simply scheduling these special Sundays probably will do little to increase worship attendance. Ideally a special ad hoc committee of five to seven people will be organized to create, plan, and implement the unique dimensions of each special Sunday. That should include special invitations to all persons concerned. It may even mean creation of special music for the occasion.

10. Seek Pledges

Close to half of all Protestant congregations ask every member to make an estimate of giving or a pledge

A Commitment to Attendance

of financial support for the coming church year.

Which is more important—financial contributions or participation in corporate worship on Sunday morning? If you conclude worship attendance is the more important of the two, it will be easy to understand why a growing number of congregations are asking all members to make an advance commitment on the number of Sundays they expect to be present during the coming year. This is an especially useful concept in those congregations that see themselves as voluntary associations and in those where the worship-attendance-to-membership ratio is below 60 percent on the average Sunday.

Asking people to make an advance commitment on their attendance by signing a pledge card is a simple means of increasing attendance by 2 to 5 percent.

A greater impact requires more work. One approach is to keep a comprehensive and accurate attendance record every Sunday. If your attendance averages more than eighty to a hundred, you may need a redundant system in which at least three *different* sources (cards in the pew, a check of the membership roster by an usher or a choir member who knows everyone, a review by the minister, the use of mailboxes for the distribution of bulletins) are used to increase the chances of complete coverage. At least a few congregations ask everyone to deposit a name tag in a box on the way out so they can be arranged in alphabetical order on the name tag racks. This box of name tags can be used to check attendance. Once a quarter (or once a month?) a letter is sent to every member comparing their pledge attendance with reality. Thus the comparison is between a self-generated goal, rather than an externally imposed goal, and reality.

Another question on that pledge card could read, "How many friends, relatives, neighbors, or colleagues from work will you introduce to our church next year by bringing them to worship with you?"

11. Encourage Mutual Accountability

A somewhat similar approach is widely used today in continuing education experiences for adults. Each person signing up for a program or course scheduled over several weeks often is asked two questions. For whom will you accept responsibility for making sure they attend every class? Who will be responsible for your attendance? When two people agree to accept the mutual accountability for each other, the chances they will attend each session increase substantially.

A parallel is on the first Sunday of the year (in some congregations this is the second Sunday in September) when members are asked to sign mutual accountability cards. Each agrees to be responsible for the other person's attendance every week.

Music Programs

12. Evaluate the Music

This alternative is saved for last in this section to provide the cowards with the chance to choose a less dangerous course of action. At least six aspects of the Sunday morning music should be examined to determine if they influence attendance.

The first, of course, is the opening hymn. Ideally that will be a joyous hymn that can be sung with enthusiasm. When people know the words and the tune of a hymn they find it easy to sing. Since so many pastors are overly educated, left-brained, rational, and systematic creatures who select hymns on the basis of their theology, it may be more appropriate to ask someone with an ear for the melody to choose at least that opening hymn. One pastor alternates between asking her husband and her secretary to pick the opening hymn.

Second, if children are expected to be in attendance, at least one hymn that is meaningful to children and one they can join in the singing will be chosen. If children leave before the sermon, their hymn may need to be the opening one.

Third, if the congregation displays a large degree of diversity in preferences in music, it may be wise to attempt to satisfy three or four groups rather than plan all the music that will be favorably received by one group and ignored or disliked by two or three other groups in the congregation.

Fourth, and this may be highly controversial in your church, paid section leaders in the choir may be justified on the basis of a superior performance, but paid singers rarely are compatible with a large choir and/or an increase in attendance.

Fifth, the music should enhance the feeling of a fast-paced service, not slow it down.

Finally, if your attendance averages more than 160 at Sunday morning worship, you should expect (a) two or more music groups on at least thirty Sundays a year and (b) a choir every Sunday. If your attendance averages over three hundred fifty on Sunday morning, you should expect at least three different music groups on forty Sundays a year (four or five if you have two or three services on Sunday morning).

Now, as you reflect on the corporate worship experiences in your congregation, what else should be done to make them more attractive and meaningful?

Another approach is to shift the focus from the worship experience to the schedule, but that requires another chapter.

2 REVIEW THE SCHEDULE

If we go to two services on Sunday morning, that will split our congregation in two groups, those who come to the early service and those who attend at the later hour," declared Herman Lansford in an angry tone of voice. "The fellowship and spirit of caring in this church will be ruined. I'm against it!"

"I'm with you, Herman," added Ethel Griffin. "The sanctuary is filled now only on three or four Sundays a year. If we add an early service, the people who attend at that hour will rattle around like peas in a bushel basket."

"That's exactly the way I feel about it," agreed Paul Bochte. "Let's wait until we fill the place for three or four months in a row before we start talking about two services."

"You don't expect the choir to sing at both services, do you?" questioned Susan Hill, a member of the seventeen-voice choir. "I would, but I'm sure most of the others wouldn't."

"We're having a hard enough time now getting ushers for one service," complained Tom McGuire, who headed the usher corps. "Where would we find enough ushers for two services?"

"What would that schedule do to the Sunday school?" asked Harry Nelson, the Sunday school superintendent. "Would that mean we would have to cut back on the time available for Sunday school?"

"I just don't think you'll find many people in this community willing to get up early on Sunday morning to come to an eight-thirty service," reflected Jack Kingman. "I think a lot of people like to sleep in on Sunday morning, and I'm afraid you'll have a very small crowd at that early service."

"It's simply beyond me why anyone would propose such an idea," declared Neva Murphy. "It sounds to me like a plot by someone who is attempting to undermine the unity and harmony of our church and to force our people to choose up sides on what clearly will be a divisive issue."

To the casual reader these comments may appear to be the typical reactions to a proposal to expand the Sunday morning schedule to two services. That is true, but that is not the crucial significance of these objections. It will be more helpful if these statements are perceived in a larger context as (a) the normal and predictable responses to a new idea when it is first presented and (b) the natural response to a proposal that is widely viewed as a radical change from the status quo.

The temptation is to focus on the merits of the proposal for a change to offering two worship experiences on Sunday morning as a means of increasing church attendance. That is the first subject to be discussed later in this chapter, but the underlying issue is change. How does one introduce and secure acceptance of new ideas that may be widely viewed as proposals for radical change? That is the theme of the last few pages of this book, but the key point that must be made here is the primary focus should be on the process of planned change from within an organization, not on the content of the proposed course of action.

The natural and predictable responses to any new idea the first time it is presented tend to fall into seven overlapping categories. The first is to explain why *that* would not work. The second is to explain why *that* would not work *here* in our situation. The third is to explain why *that* would not work *here now*. The fourth is to affirm the status quo. The fifth is to identify insurmountable obstacles. The sixth is to begin to build a list of those who will oppose it and the seventh is to attack the competence or integrity of those who propose the change. (All normal paranoids will understand this very easily.)

Thus the initial focal point in suggesting changes often should not be on the proposed course of action, but rather on arousing discontent with the status quo. This can be illustrated by five different introductions of the same basic point.

The first, and the one most likely to receive strong opposition, is, "Let's change the Sunday morning schedule to include two worship services with Sunday school between the two."

The second would be to challenge people with a new vision of what could be, "Would you like to see our Sunday morning attendance increase by at least 15 percent over the next year or so?"

A third would be to build on the past by asking, "Some of you can remember when we averaged close to 160 people at Sunday morning worship. It's now down to about 135 or 140. Would you like to see it climb back up to what it used to be?"

A fourth could be to build on minor or latent discontent by redefining the issue. "Several of you have commented that our attendance on Sunday morning is not what it should be or could be. One way of increasing it would be to go to two services on Sunday morning. What do you think? Should the first service begin at eight-fifteen or eight-thirty?"

A fifth approach assumes the existence of a significant degree of discontent with the status quo and frames the question to focus the debate on the *when* rather than the *if* of change. "We've talked at different times about the need to increase church attendance. One way of doing that would be to offer people the choice of an early service or a late service. If we decide to do that, what do you think would be the best time to make the change? The first Sunday in Lent? The first Sunday in June? The first Sunday in September?"

Each of the last four approaches is likely to evoke less immediate opposition than the first. Therefore, as you reflect on changes in the schedule as a means of increasing church attendance, a critical factor may be on how you word the proposal.

Now let us leave strategy and tactics and examine five possibilities for increasing church attendance by altering the schedule.

1. Offer More Services

Approximately four out of five congregations that report a change from one worship experience on

Sunday morning to two add this was followed by an *increase* of 10 to 20 percent in the average attendance. In one out of five the change, usually for distinctive local reasons, was not followed by any significant increase in attendance.

Increasing the number of services!
—FRIAR JUCK

Approximately three out of four churches that have cut back their Sunday morning schedule from two services to one report that this was followed by a *decrease* in attendance. In one out of four, again apparently for local reasons, the change was not followed by a decrease in attendance, and in a few churches attendance actually increased following that cutback.

In other words, while no guarantee can be offered, the evidence suggests that a change in the number of services often will be followed by a predictable change in attendance.

While these are not the only reasons for changing to two services, four factors do stand out as common motivations for offering that schedule.

The first, and one of the most common is sometimes referred to as "the 80 percent rule." Whenever your average attendance exceeds 80 percent of your capacity, you probably are encouraging people to stay away. This includes first-time visitors who do not want to be perceived as a problem and therefore do not return. It also may cause many members to reduce the frequency of their own attendance as a subconscious response to the fact that on many Sundays the nave is crowded.

It must be remembered that if the typical congregation averages, for example, 150 people at worship for the entire year, it must have at least fifteen or twenty Sundays a year when attendance approaches 180 or 190. That is necessary to offset the low attendance on many Sundays if the attendance is going to average 150 for the entire year. That means if the building can comfortably accommodate 190 at worship (including the choir), the leaders will be faced with four alternatives when attendance averages more than 150. One is to build a larger facility. A second is to expand by remodeling. A third is to accept the fact that the frequency of attendance probably will drop and many first-time visitors will leave feeling, "They don't need us," and not return. The fourth alternative is to change to two services on Sunday morning.[1]

Some will argue that the time to expand to two services already has arrived when the average attendance exceeds 75 percent of the capacity. It also should be noted that the word "capacity" does not refer to the architect's stated figure which often means crowding. Most Americans prefer 24 to 28 inches of space in the pew, not 20 or 22 inches. They also prefer

---

[1]A frequently suggested fifth alternative of "starting a new church out there to relieve some of the pressure on us" probably will not produce the desired results since people attracted by the challenge of helping pioneer a new mission frequently are not the same type of people who would be interested in joining a long-established congregation that does not want to reach and serve more people.

to have chairs at least three or four inches apart, not close together.

A second common reason for expanding to two worship services is illustrated by the congregation that includes many younger families who want their children to attend worship but also serves several articulate mature adults who object to the distraction of noisy children. (See point 2 in the next chapter.) A widespread response is to create an image of a "family service" at one hour and the "traditional service" at the other hour.

In many recreational areas the two-service schedule was introduced to enable the golfers, the boaters, the folks who like to go fishing, the tennis players, and the hikers to attend church early in the morning and have the rest of the day free for fun and games.

Finally, one of the historic reasons for two Sunday morning worship services in American Protestantism was to offer one service in the mother language and the other in English. That pattern largely disappeared in the period from 1917 to 1942, but began to reappear in the 1960s as more and more Anglo congregations began to welcome the new immigrants from Latin America and the Pacific Rim.

Today these reasons are overshadowed by another consideration in evaluating the Sunday morning schedule. That is the increasing diversity among the members of a large number of long-established congregations.

"We tried the idea of offering a contemporary service at nine o'clock and a traditional service at eleven," explained a minister from Oregon, "but we ended up with all of the Democrats coming to the first service and the Republicans coming at eleven. We decided that wasn't good, so we now offer identical services at nine and eleven."

That illustrates those famous seven words that should not be overlooked when designing the Sunday morning schedule. *You never can do only one thing.* Every change has consequences beyond those that were anticipated. With this warning it is appropriate to look at another means of increasing church attendance.

2. *Offer More Choices*

Perhaps the most widely followed schedule that includes two worship services is worship with either no special music or a children's choir or youth choir at the first hour followed by Sunday church school followed by the full-scale second service with the adult choir. Usually this means the services are close to carbon copies and frequently one bulletin is prepared for both services. The second service may be a little longer, the sermon has had the benefit of a dress rehearsal and the anthem may be different. Essentially, however, the services are the same and the real choices are (a) the hour, (b) the special music, (c) the size of the crowd, and (d) the choice of who the fellow worshipers will be.

If the congregation includes a fairly diverse collection of people in terms of (a) where they are on their journey of faith, (b) denominational heritage, (c) generational differences, (d) theological orientation, (e) preferences in music, and (f) their definition of priorities in describing the reasons for the existence of a worshiping community, it may be useful to expand the range of

choices. If should be
added that these differ-
ences will tend to be
greater in (a) the long-
established church
founded before 1960
than in the new congre-
gation, (b) the congre-
gation served by six or
seven ministers over the
past four decades than
the one served by the
same pastor for two or
three decades, (c) the
numerically growing

IN ORDER TO BE
ALL THINGS
TO ALL PEOPLE...

CHURCH SCHOOL   SPACE   SPECIAL MUSIC   FORMAL   CASUAL

Differing Worship
Services

—FRIAR TUCK

congregation than in the one on a plateau or shrinking in
size, (d) the one that resembles a voluntary association
rather than the high expectation covenant community,
and (e) the one that draws at least a fourth of its
members from each of three different generations.

One set of choices was mentioned in the first chapter:
offer a choice of preachers. Others could be different
liturgies, or orders of worship for the two services, a
different style of preaching, or one service might place a
greater emphasis on lay participation while the other
may be led by the pastor. One could be "formal" and one
could be "contemporary." One may include the Lord's
Supper every Sunday and the other only once a month
or once a quarter. One may include an altar call while the
other does not. One may have the sermon delivered
from the pulpit while at the other hour the preacher
comes out of the chancel to walk among the people while
delivering the sermon. One could be in the sanctuary

while the other could be in the church parlor or chapel or fellowship hall to accommodate a smaller crowd. One could include the hymns the people enjoy singing while at the other hour the people are asked to sing the hymns the minister was taught in seminary to choose for corporate worship. It is not uncommon for the early service to be widely understood to be the hour when casual dress is appropriate while the dress code still applies at the later hour.

In many congregations the degree of differences will be a reflection both of the diversity within the membership and of the desire to increase attendance.

Four critical tests of a willingness to legitimatize and recognize diversity are (a) the decision to prepare two different bulletins, (b) the decision to organize two different adult choirs with two different directors, (c) the decision to schedule several large group events every year to bring people together from the two (or three) different services, and (d) the relaxed and positive response received by the unanticipated consequences of the decision to offer people a wider range of choices.

A growing variation of this same theme of expanding the range of choices as a means of increasing worship attendance is the alternative service designed to accommodate the millions of people who cannot attend on Sunday mornings. Perhaps the three most common variations of this are (a) Saturday evening, (b) late Sunday afternoon, frequently to match a change of shifts at a nearby hospital or the closing of the shopping mall at five o'clock Sunday, or (c) Thursday evening.

With several notable exceptions these alternative

services tend to attract an average of fewer than thirty-five worshipers.

One response to that pattern has been to build a stronger sense of a distinctive theme, such as music, into that Saturday evening service or to focus more sharply on a clearly identified clientele such as young adults or the formerly married or the lonely or the remarried.

Another response has been to expand the number of reasons why people might attend. In several churches, for example, people begin to gather before six o'clock for a carry-in dinner that begins at six. This is followed by worship at seven, study at eight-fifteen, and dessert and fellowship about nine-thirty or ten.

This leads us into another approach to increasing worship attendance by changing the schedule.

3. Expand the Schedule

One of the changes in our society that began to appear in the late 1960s and emerged full blown in the 1980s has been the rapidly growing number of people who do not eat breakfast at home. Examples include the farmers' pickup trucks lined up outside the small town restaurant, the number of people who eat breakfast in an airplane, the phenomenal increase in business breakfast meetings, the growing number of breakfast prayer groups in downtown office buildings, and the husband who leaves after his wife already has left and buys his breakfast on the way to work. The trade journals that service restaurant owners repeatedly emphasize that one way to increase profits is to offer breakfast.

WE'LL SHOW UP WHEN YOU SHOW UP!

WELCOME TO THE LATE, LATE WORSHIP SERVICE

Expand the schedule!

— FRIAR TUCK

One expression of this recent trend has been the growing number of churches that begin the Sunday morning schedule with breakfast.

Before discussing the details of that alternative, it must be emphasized that offering breakfast is not the basic issue. The crucial question to be raised in any discussion about expanding the schedule can be expressed in seven words. *What do we expect of our people?* Do we expect members to come for one, two, three, four, or five hours on Sunday morning? While it is impossible to demonstrate a cause and effect relationship, it is worth noting that the churches with the highest average attendance-at-worship-to-membership ratio are the ones (a) most likely to expect members to be present for *at least* two hours on Sunday morning and (b) most likely to have their Sunday school attendance approach or exceed their worship attendance. Thus when the subject of breakfast is introduced, the focus should be on expectations, not menus!

A common pattern in those churches that have expanded the schedule to four or five hours is for the first people to arrive before seven o'clock on Sunday morning to begin the preparations for breakfast. Around seven a few people straggle in for breakfast and conversation. A little later the members of that adult

class that meets over breakfast for an hour or two come in, fill their trays, and go off to their classroom. They may be followed by the members of the choir who will sing for the first service and the latecomers who arrive just in time to have breakfast before the first service. Several pastors report this period of sixty to ninety minutes is one of the most productive hours in the week for pastoral care.

One or two adult classes may meet concurrently with the first service. (The most effective means of organizing a new adult class at that early hour is to have a minister teach it.) A second worship experience may or may not be offered concurrently with the Sunday church hour and one or more adult classes along with one or two Sunday school classes for teenagers and/or young adults may be offered at that hour. (It should be noted that the number of thirty-two-year-olds in America will reach a peak for this century in the 1988–94 era and many of that generation are returning to church while in their early thirties.) That second teenage Sunday school class at the last hour may be offered for the high school age youth who are not interested in socializing with the people in the class that meets an hour earlier or it may be for the high school youth choir that sings at the middle service or it may be for the juniors and seniors who teach during the Sunday school hour.

Obviously a schedule as complicated as this probably would be of little interest to leaders in congregations averaging fewer than 115 to 140 at Sunday morning worship unless these leaders were determined to attract more members as well as to increase the worship attendance-to-membership ratio.

One of the important advantages of this schedule is that it enables some members to teach in the Sunday school, participate in an adult class, and also attend worship. In those congregations where the building allows this to happen, the choir that sings at the first service may be in Sunday school at the next hour and rehearse during the last hour. This schedule also is compatible with the priorities of those parents who want their children to be in both worship and Sunday school.

Finally, it should be noted that several churches have found that the responsibility for preparing and serving breakfast can be an effective central organizing principle for creating a large and cohesive men's fellowship. That also may be a means of guaranteeing an extensive and attractive menu every week!

4. Create a New Congregation

"Would you folks like to join me and support me in a two-year experiment to increase our membership?" the pastor of a hundred-year-old congregation averaging between seventy-five and eighty at the eleven o'clock Sunday morning worship service asked a group of leaders in an informal gathering one Tuesday evening.

"What do you have in mind?" came the reply.

"What I would like to do for the next two years would be to have you reduce your expectations of me as your pastor to half-time responsibilities, but you would continue to pay me on a full-time basis. I would devote one-half my time every week to serving as your pastor and spend the other half of my time organizing a new congregation out of the people in this community who

are not actively involved in the life of any congregation. I would follow the same principles and procedures as if I were off somewhere else organizing a new mission except (a) I would be doing this on a half-time basis and (b) when the time came to launch our first worship service, we would meet in this building at eight-thirty on Sunday morning. That way we would be done before the ten o'clock Sunday school hour and if any of the members of this new congregation wanted to stay for Sunday school, they could do so. I need a two-year commitment to make sure I have sufficient time to get this congregation organized with its own sense of identity before we begin to talk about combining that group with our present membership."

This is a radical and, to some people, a threatening idea. A far more common and less threatening proposal is when the pastor asks for half-time status and full-time compensation in order to go back to school for a year or two or three. In today's world additional formal education apparently is less threatening to many local church leaders than an intensive effort to reach more people with the Good News that Jesus Christ is Lord and Savior!

The central reason for such a proposal, rather than to attempt to combine unchurched people into a long-established congregation, is that the majority of adults are more receptive to a request to help pioneer something new rather than to respond to an invitation to join an ongoing and often exclusionary group. This same principle explains why it is easier to enlist people in a new adult class than to recruit new members for a long-established class. It also explains why it often is easier to organize new circles in the women's

organization than to persuade younger women to join the long-established groups.

In at least a few cases the pastor concluded this plan had the best chances of success by scheduling worship for the first year or two in another place. This reinforced the concept of helping pioneer the new.

While this alternative has been followed more often in smaller congregations than in large ones (partly because the number of small congregations is six times the number of large churches), a few large congregations have used this same basic system in asking an associate minister to organize a new congregation that would meet during the Sunday school hour. In either case an essential goal is that at least 98 percent of the participants will be drawn from among people who currently are not actively involved in the life of any worshiping congregation. If the "sponsoring" congregation supplies more than one or two people, they will tend to fill the leadership positions, keep the newcomers from feeling like influential pioneers, and create a clone of the sponsor.

Finally, it should be clear that this concept will have the greatest appeal to the pastor who possesses entrepreneurial gifts, likes people, knows how to manage his or her time, and enjoys leading a two- or three-track life.

5. Analyze the Impact of the Location in the Time Zone and Life-Styles

Perhaps the three most widely neglected factors in designing the Sunday morning schedule are (a) location in a time zone, (b) changing life-styles, and (c) the National Football League. These are interrelated, but they can be discussed separately.

One basic generalization is that as one goes from east to west, the hour at which the largest number of people gather for worship is earlier. The eleven o'clock service still draws large crowds on the Atlantic seaboard but the biggest crowds may be at the nine-thirty or ten o'clock worship on the West Coast.

Second, in the North during the winter it is more difficult to attract people to an early service in the western end of a time zone (especially in the western end of that wide Central time zone) than it is in the eastern end of the same time zone.

Third, time budget surveys going back to the 1930s indicate that today people are spending more time shopping, less time reading books and magazines, more time in the journey to work and less time in bed. Today's generation of people in the 35-54 age bracket get up earlier in the morning than was true of the same age group in the 1930s. One obvious implication is an earlier hour for worship will be more attractive today than it was in the 1930s.

Fourth, more people are eating far more meals out today than previously. This can be seen most clearly in the Southeast where many ministers pronounce the benediction at eleven-thirty or eleven-forty-five or eleven-fifty to enable their members to beat the Baptists or Methodists to the front of the cafeteria lines.

Fifth, a great many adults today plan to take a trip or go to a recreational spot after worship and thus they prefer an earlier hour for worship, especially in the North during the summer.

Sixth, the National Football League and its televised games are far more influential in determining people's schedules than major league baseball has ever been. Again this is more apparent in the West than in the East.

Seventh, the increasing number of divorced (and sometimes remarried) parents who share custody of their children does encourage some to prefer an earlier hour for Sunday school and worship.

Eighth, the almost complete scrapping of Sunday "blue laws" has made the early Sunday morning hour or the Sunday evening service or the Saturday evening worship attractive to the growing number of people who work Sundays.

How do these influence the factors that determine your schedule in your community?

Perhaps the umbrella under which that discussion should be conducted is the larger one of basic policies rather than the narrower one of the Sunday morning schedule.

3 WHAT ARE YOUR OPERATIONAL POLICIES?

About five years ago I realized we had to take a second look at our policy on weddings," explained the forty-two-year-old Texas pastor. "For at least twenty years the policy here has been to charge nonmembers for the use of the sanctuary and the fellowship hall, but there was no charge for members.

"Eight years ago this young woman moved here to teach in the public schools and began to worship with us. Before the year was out she was helping teach the third- and fourth-grade class in our Sunday school. From late August through May she rarely missed church. After school was out, she returned to her home in Boston to live with her parents while she worked on a master's degree in summer school. When I asked her if she wanted to transfer her membership, she told me she expected to be here for only a few years and preferred to keep her membership in her home church. By the end of the second year she was one of the most valued Sunday school teachers and she also helped in several other programs.

"Well, to make a long story short, during her fourth year she and a fellow teacher decided to get married. He wasn't a member of any church, but occasionally came to worship with her. He had grown up in a town about sixty miles from here. Since all their mutual friends, as well as most of his relatives, live in central Texas, they decided to be married here rather than in Boston. Late one Saturday afternoon they came in to ask me if I would be willing to officiate at their wedding. An hour earlier

I had performed a wedding for another couple. She was and still is a member, but she had not been in church on Sunday morning more than five times since she graduated from high school. Her parents are members, but rarely show up for worship except perhaps at Easter and Christmas. Since the bride and her parents are members, we did not even consider charging them for the use of the building.

"An hour later I am talking about the wedding of one of our most valuable volunteers, but since she was not a member, the policy stated that she would have to pay for the use of the building. When I took this to the trustees, they immediately declared we should waive the nonmember fee in this case. One of the trustees, however, questioned the whole policy and urged that we reconsider it. He argued the old policy emphasized real estate and finances rather than evangelism and that it was basically an exclusionary policy.

"As a result our current policy does not focus on charging for the use of the building, but rather on people and evangelism. After several meetings we developed a new policy that makes no charge to anyone who uses the building. The only requirement for being married here now are (a) the minister must be willing to perform the wedding for that particular couple, (b) one or both parties must have attended worship here for at least six Sundays in the three months before the wedding is scheduled, or (c) one or both parties must be from a family who are members. The last provision is to accommodate the bride-to-be who moved away after graduation from high school, but wants to be married in the church where her parents are now members. We have several families who have moved here since their youngest child graduated from high school and the daughter, who may never have lived here, still wants to be married here because of her parents."

"If I understand correctly," inquired the visitor, "you made this new policy five years ago. How do you feel about it today?"

"It was a great idea!" exclaimed the Texas pastor. "I was taught in seminary that a minister was ethically obligated to require several counseling sessions with a couple before agreeing to officiate at the wedding. Well, David and Vera Mace blew that concept right out of the water a few years ago when they declared that was a waste of time. Second, as this one trustee pointed out to us, our old policy was really somewhere between dumb and exclusionary since it focused on real estate and money rather than on evangelism. Our new policy emphasizes the centrality of worship and invites people to worship with us rather than encouraging them to pay money instead of coming to church. Finally, the proof of the pudding is in the eating, and during the past five years we have received at least two dozen members who are regular attenders today as a result of this new policy."

This account illustrates one of the seven basic areas

of congregational life that should be explored by any congregation seeking to increase attendance at Sunday morning worship.

The umbrella question is, Do the operational policies in your congregation tend to encourage or discourage people from participating in the corporate worship of God with your congregation? This can be illustrated by looking at seven specific policies.

1. Change the Policy on Weddings

What is your policy in regard to weddings? Does your current policy encourage nonmembers to pay money for using the building? Or does your current policy encourage nonmembers to come and worship with your people in the expectation, to use an old cliché, "Try it, you'll like it!"

2. Encourage Children to Worship God

Perhaps the most influential single policy in regard to the size of the crowd on Sunday morning concerns the attendance of children.

While no one has been able to prove a cause-and-effect relationship, numerous surveys have revealed that parents of young children who bring their children to worship attend church more frequently than do parents with children of the same age who are not accompanied by their children at worship.

One reason for this pattern may be that the parents who bring their children to worship may be attempting

Children's Sermons

NOW HERE'S WHAT I WANT YOUR PARENTS TO KNOW...

The messages tend to be brief, lucid, visual and concrete and recalled ! — FRIAR TUCK

to model acceptable behavior. Or it may be that the churches that encourage parents to bring their children to worship project a higher level of expectations to people than do those congregations that do not encourage children to attend worship. Or it may be that those congregations that expect everyone to be present for both Sunday school and corporate worship simply have more appeal to committed people.

Whatever the reasons may be, it is obvious that mutually reinforcing factors are at work which will increase the number of people present for worship on the typical Sunday morning if the policy is to encourage the attendance of children.

The most obvious consequence is that if the frequency of attendance by parents increases, the average attendance will increase. The second is that attendance obviously will be higher in the congregation that averages 140 adults plus forty children at worship than it will be in the church that averages 140 adults plus five or six children. A third factor is that most (not all) congregations that encourage children to attend worship also expect both parents and children to be in Sunday school. That reinforces the attractiveness of Sunday morning for many people.

A fourth and far more subtle factor that many

ministers are loath to discuss is that some adults do not follow and/ or comprehend the sermon. However, if children are present and a children's sermon is given, the possibility of the adults hearing a brief, lucid, visual, and concrete message that they can recall several days later is increased. In many congregations the one time when the

minister has 100 percent of the attention of the people in the room is while delivering that brief, visual, right-brained, and simple message to the children.

A fifth reason why inviting children may increase worship attendance is that some of the first-time visitors who gave birth to their first child a year or two ago may find this more attractive than feeling conspicuous because they are the only ones in the room accompanied by a young child. In reflecting on this it is worth noting that in 1986, 1.6 million women gave birth to their first child compared to fewer than 1.2 million at the peak of the baby boom of 1956–62 and compared to 1.4 million mothers in 1977. Parents with their first child tend to very self-conscious of their new status and role.

A sixth and potentially very powerful reason why this can be an important policy in regard to worship attendance lies in the distinction between attendance and participation. Those congregations that encourage the *participation* of children in Sunday morning worship often contend that in addition to making this a more *meaningful* experience for the child, the participation of the children also increases the attractiveness of that experience for adults. The range of participation includes the children's sermon, a children's choir, older children serving as acolytes or ushers or greeters or receiving the offering, or liturgical dance.

Another subtle reason this policy can influence church attendance is reflected in the debate over "the one-hour package." Many people contend that it is essential, if the goal is to attract parents of young children, to offer worship at the same hour as Sunday school. In addition to undercutting the educational ministry and the group life of the church and in making it difficult for many teachers to both teach and attend worship, this schedule often tends to encourage erratic attendance by the parents in worship and by the children in the Sunday school.

The policy of encouraging all children to share in corporate worship may be the most effective means of removing the "one-hour package" from the agenda of current issues.

In scores of churches an influential reason for encouraging children to participate in corporate worship is a product of the opposition of a significant number of mature adults. Some of these objectors have a hearing impediment which means they simply cannot hear the words of the prayer or the sermon if a noisy child is nearby. Others are distracted by a restless child. A few object when the child sitting behind them runs a small vehicle over their head during the silent meditation. If the sanctuary has a sloping floor, many will study their watches to determine how long it takes a marble to roll from the back pew to the chancel railing.

The only effective response to what are truly legitimate objections to inviting noisy children to attend worship is to offer two services *every* Sunday morning, one which is designed to attract parents with young children and one which is strictly an adult experience. As was pointed out in an earlier section, the shift to two services often results in 15 to 20 percent increase in worship attendance. Encouraging noisy children to participate in corporate worship is one way of building a support group for a two-service schedule.

Finally, and most important, what do you believe about the importance of helping children learn to worship God? That really should be the central question when this issue is discussed.

3. Cancel the Summer Slump

A widespread policy in thousands of congregations during the third quarter of this century was to reduce the schedule during the summer, perhaps give the choir a vacation of two or three months and maybe cut back on Sunday school during July and August. Frequently the pastor would be on vacation for several Sundays and many larger churches offered only one worship service, rather than two or three, during the summer.

In several communities two congregations would schedule joint services for July and August. A common pattern was for both congregations to meet in the Presbyterian church during July while the Presbyterian minister was on vacation. The Methodist minister would lead the worship service and the Methodist choir would sing the anthem. In August the pattern would be reversed and both congregations would worship in the Methodist building with the Presbyterian minister and the Presbyterian choir leading in worship.

The widespread assumption was that many people would be gone during the summer and a summer slump was inevitable. In recent years hundreds of leaders have questioned this assumption and suggested that what really was happening was a self-fulfilling prophecy. The prediction of a summer slump was fulfilled by the lowering of expectations and the cutback in programming. Dozens of churches have demonstrated the validity of this by canceling the summer slump with the result that worship attendance in July and August is approximately the same as in May or November.

What is the operational policy in your congregation in regard to the summer slump? Are you content with that policy?

More and more congregations are discovering the summer slump can be eliminated by (a) continuing the full schedule throughout the summer, (b) perhaps adding an extra worship experience early Sunday morning or on Saturday evening, (c) scheduling a music group (not a soloist or duet!) for every service, (d) expecting the pastor to be in the pulpit on all but one or two Sundays during the summer, (e) planning a special program or event for each Sunday during the summer, (f) offering a choice of Sunday school classes every week, (g) scheduling one attractive evening event during the week for every week (one church schedules a Thursday evening ice cream social every week during the summer called "Sundaes on Thursday"), (h) in

various other ways expanding the program rather than cutting back on it, and (i) undergirding all of this with an effective advertising program.

In addition to increasing, rather than decreasing worship attendance during the summer, another big reason for canceling the summer slump is that summer is the peak of the church shopping season. Two-thirds of all families who change their place of residence do so during the one-third of the year from mid-May to mid-September. The church with a full summer schedule is more attractive to the first-time church shopper than the congregation with an abbreviated program.

Overlapping the policy in regard to the summer slump is the policy on the basic Sunday morning schedule.

Does your congregation change the schedule for the summer by shifting to early hours? Or does your congregation follow the same schedule for all twelve months of the year? What is the policy?

Three generalizations merit consideration. First, people are creatures of habit. Changing the schedule twice or more a year can have a negative impact on worship attendance as people are expected to learn new habits. Second, it is easier to communicate a clear message with a simple schedule in the Yellow Pages

than a two-schedule for-
mat. Third, if changes
are to be made, try to
change only by addition,
not by altering the exist-
ing schedule. Thus an
additional early worship
service might be offered
on Easter Sunday and/or
during the summer
without altering the
basic schedule.

Scheduling
Sunday school
before worship
usually has
a positive impact!

—FRIAR TUCK

It also is important
that the first-time visitor
in July or August gain a
clear understanding of what the fall schedule will be
during that first visit. The easiest way to do that is to
have the same schedule.

4. Review the Sunday Morning Sequence

Most congregations offer a schedule with Sunday
school followed by worship. Others schedule worship
first followed by Sunday school.

Experience suggests people who come to Sunday
school usually are comfortable with the idea of "staying
for church" but for some it is tempting to leave following
worship rather than stay for Sunday school. Scheduling
Sunday school first, followed by worship, usually has a
positive impact on worship.

What is your policy? Does worship follow Sunday
school or does Sunday school follow worship?

If worship follows Sunday school, you offer people two reasons to get out of bed and come to worship. One is to come to Sunday school. The second is, "As long as we're here, let's stay for church." When worship is first, you may be offering only one reason for getting up early.

5. Review Policy on Frequency of Lord's Supper

Two generalizations can be offered in regard to the frequency of Holy Communion. First, back in the 1950s the common pattern in several denominations was to offer the Lord's Supper once a quarter. Today, in many of these same congregations Holy Communion is celebrated once a month or perhaps even weekly.

Second, in some congregations worship attendance is consistently up on those Sundays when the schedule includes Holy Communion. In other congregations worship attendance is consistently down on Communion Sunday.

What is your policy on this subject and what are the consequences of that policy? Are you satisfied with the current policy or should it be changed?

An increasingly common policy is to offer people a choice by building the first worship service around the Lord's Supper on every Sunday of the year and offering Holy Communion only once a month or once a quarter at the second service. This is an additional argument in support of two different services and is especially relevant to those congregations that draw members from a variety of denominational backgrounds including Roman Catholic.

6. Expand Your Advertising Budget

What is your congregation's policy on advertising?

This can affect new member enlistment as well as attendance. A useful rule of thumb for congregations seriously interested in expanding their outreach and in increasing worship attendance is to allocate at least 5 percent of the budget for advertising and public relations.

The most productive channels usually are (a) direct mail, (b) the telephone, (c) television, (d) "story" advertisements in the newspaper on Monday through Thursday, (e) radio, and (f) the shopping "throwaway."

A two-track system of direct mail advertising can be an effective means of increasing worship attendance. One track is directed at members and the other track is directed at potential members and potential visitors.

Who formulates the policy on advertising in your congregation? What criteria are used in developing that policy? Who implements the policy?

7. When Is the Fellowship Hour?

A common schedule in many congregations calls for Sunday school at nine or nine-thirty followed by a fellowship-with-refreshments period for approximately thirty minutes followed by corporate worship at ten-thirty or eleven. In many larger congregations this basic schedule has been expanded to include an early worship service that is concluded before the Sunday school hour.

This basic schedule has many attractive features. It encourages people to attend both Sunday school and worship. It enables the teacher in the Sunday school to share in worship. The half hour following Sunday school provides times for the choir to assemble, robe, and warm up. That half hour gives the minister a chance to offer a lot of pastoral care to several people in a brief period of time. It also gives "the regulars" the opportunity to relax and reinforce their relationships with one another.

The serious flaw in that schedule is that first-time visitors (a) usually plan to arrive just before that worship service scheduled for ten-thirty or eleven, (b) may have difficulty finding a convenient parking space because the people participating in that fellowship period often do not leave until it is too late for anyone else to use their parking space (this is most serious, obviously, in those congregations that offer an early service before Sunday school or in those churches where many adults attend Sunday school but depart before worship), and (c) miss the warm welcome they might have received during that fellowship period.

One response to that dilemma is to require all first-time visitors to come in time for Sunday school or at least a half hour before worship. That may be difficult to enforce.

An alternative response could be to arrange the schedule so corporate worship is concluded by eleven forty-five and followed by a fellowship period. This is especially important from September through December west of Indiana where National Football League games are on television somewhere between eight o'clock and noon. This also is an important. point for those churches expecting to increase the number of church shoppers who return after that first visit.

As you review the operational policies of your congregation, do you see changes in any of these areas that might influence the attendance on Sunday morning?

4   THE POWER OF PROGRAM

Back in the 1950s the most effective course of action for a minister to follow in organizing a new congregation was to call at every household in what was defined as that new mission's service area. Today direct mail advertising has replaced calling as the most cost effective tactic in an overall strategy for organizing a new congregation.

Back in the 1950s the most effective approach to attracting new members to a long-established congregation was for the pastor to call on all new families moving into that community. Today in a majority of congregations excellent and relevant preaching and an attractive program are more effective tools for attracting new members to the long-established congregation than is pastoral calling.

Back in the 1950s pastoral calling was the most effective means for increasing church attendance, especially in congregations averaging under two hundred at Sunday morning worship. It is still useful today, but much more expensive in terms of time, energy, and frustration. The two-income household and the sharp increase in the number of one-person households has undercut the effectiveness of calling. (In 1880, 3 percent of all American households included only one person and another 10 percent consisted of two people. By 1950 the proportion of one-person households had climbed to only 11 percent and in 1970 it was still 17 percent. By 1985, 24 percent of all households in the United States consisted of only one person and another 32 percent consisted of two people.

In one century the proportion of one- or two-person households had quadrupled from 13 percent to 56 percent.)

One consequence of the decrease in both the practicality and the effectiveness of pastoral calling has been a remarkable decline in the number of allegations of proselytizing or "sheep stealing." Another has been the enhanced role of programming both in attracting new members and in influencing the frequency of attendance of members.

A third consequence is the erosion of the advantages held by the minister with an attractive personality who also was a faithful and effective pastoral caller, but who possessed limited skills as a pulpiteer or as a program director.

Another consequence has been the emergence of the "church shopper" who visits three to ten churches over a period of months before settling on a new church home. Church shoppers now include many persons born before 1930 who, back in the 1950s or 1960s, more or less automatically picked the church located closest to their place of residence.

The growing power of program has had another consequence that has been largely overlooked. This is illustrated in the actions of the couple who were loyal and faithful members of the same congregation for several years, but when their children entered the teenage years, they left that congregation to join another church that offered a more attractive ministry with teenagers.

Several years later they changed churches again as they entered the empty nest stage of life and sought a church that had a meaningful program for people at that stage of the life cycle. Many families now change churches two or three or four times while continuing to live in the same residence.

Finally, the quality and the range of programming has become increasingly influential in reaching the generations of Americans born after World War II. They are far less likely to choose a church on the basis of its location or denominational affiliation than were their parents' generation and far more likely to choose a church on the basis of the preaching or the program or the music or the theological stance of that congregation.

While this is a highly emotional issue and provokes all kinds of ideological arguments, one consequence of the increasing power of program is that the small congregation today may find itself in a threatened position simply because it does not have the resources necessary for a full-scale program. This change, plus the erosion of denominational loyalties and the Americanization of what once were nationality parishes, means that the personality, creativity, leadership abilities, and tenure of the minister are far more influential factors in determining the future of the small urban or suburban congregation than was the case as recently as the 1960s.

If one accepts the argument that program today is a far more powerful factor in determining not only where people go to church, but also in influencing the frequency of attendance, the obvious question is, How can we utilize the power of programming to increase our worship attendance? Among the many possible responses five stand out in today's world.

1. Conceptualize a Larger Context

Instead of thinking in conventional terms about a youth fellowship or Sunday school classes or Mother's Day Out or a church picnic or occasional Bible study groups or a Men's Club or a choir, it may be useful to think in terms of larger and more inclusive terms. Four examples will illustrate this point.

Instead of thinking in terms of a high school youth group, consider the idea of creating a new ministry with families that include teenagers. This concept immediately opens the mind to contemplate specialized facets of that larger program with stepparents or one-parent households or stepchild-stepparent relationships or classes for parents who are experiencing their first encounter of living with a teenager or a sharing group for parents who are about to say farewell to the last teenager in the family.

Second, as an alternative to seeking a youth minister to build a program with the children of members, recruit a youth evangelist who will build a youth ministry largely from among teenagers not related to any worshiping community.

Instead of thinking about a weekday nursery school or Mother's Day Out, think in terms of a ministry with families that include preschool children. This opens up the possibilities of offering under one umbrella classes on parenting, a Sunday school class for parents of young children, music encounter experiences for young children, exercise classes, mutual support groups for first-time mothers, weekday Bible study groups for women, weekend camping trips, coed volleyball games, a young adult choir, an early childhood development center and a score of other components for that large package of programs.

Instead of simply debating policies on weddings (see item 1 in chapter 3), it might be more creative to think about a more comprehensive approach that would not only encourage weddings in the building, but also offer a Sunday school class for newlyweds, another class for couples in their second or subsequent marriage, bicycle trips for newlyweds, classes on becoming a stepparent or on making one family out of two households.

The larger the context used for planning program, the more points of entry for newcomers, the more places at which people can gain a sense of belonging, and the more opportunities for people to meet and make new friends. The closer a church is to the voluntary association end of that spectrum which has the high expectation churches at the other end, the more influential in determining the frequency of attendance are (a) a sense of belonging and (b) the number of friends a person has in that congregation.

2. Build Mutually Reinforcing Components

In addition to thinking in a larger frame of reference, it also is useful to plan programs so they are mutually reinforcing. One facet of that was illustrated in the previous section as in each example the various components reinforce the participants' relationships with one another and with that congregation.

A second part of this same basic concept concerns the teaching ministry of the church. It may be wise to choose teachers who will reinforce the theological perspective, the approach to biblical interpretation, and the definition of the nature of the church offered in the sermons.

Another facet of mutual reinforcement should be in program planning. Thus the program and experiences planned for the senior high youth group should be planned and publicized in a manner that causes the third-graders and the seventh-graders to think, "Gee, I can't wait until I'm old enough to be a part of that group!"

The program of the Men's Fellowship can be designed to reinforce denominational loyalties, to undergird the congregationwide sense of mission and outreach, and to reinforce the relationship between the pastor and those men.

The more the various events, experiences, and programs are mutually reinforcing, the more likely they will produce a stronger bonding of members to that fellowship. The stronger that bond, the more frequent the Sunday morning attendance.

3. *Minimize Internal Competition*

"Please don't be offended when a few of us get up and walk out about halfway through your presentation," explained a member of the Homebuilders' Sunday school class to the visiting speaker. "That should not be interpreted that we are walking out on you, but at ten-thirty we have to leave to robe and warm up with the choir for the service that begins at ten forty-five."

"If I attended every committee of which I am an ex-officio member," declared the lay leader at Wesley

United Methodist Church, "I would have to be at the church about two dozen evenings every month."

Minimize Schedule Conflicts

—FRIAR TUCK

"How in the world do they expect our kids to be in the youth choir and also help in the Sunday school when the monthly teachers' meeting is scheduled at the same hour as the rehearsal for the youth choir?" demanded the mother of a sixteen-year-old who was part of the teaching team for the third- and fourth-grade class and was also in the youth choir.

While it may be impossible to eliminate all such conflicts in scheduling, a critical component of any strategy to increase church attendance will be to minimize internal conflicts over schedule.

The most widespread example of ignoring this advice is the congregation that offers worship and Sunday school at the same hour. While that convenience package may attract some parents who want to be in worship while their children are in Sunday school, it is obvious a teacher cannot be in worship and in the classroom at the same time.

Far more serious from a long-term perspective is that schedule teaches children either (a) they are not important, or (b) corporate worship is not appropriate for them. After several years of those messages some church leaders wonder why those children "drop out of church" when they feel they are too old for Sunday school.

For those concerned solely with increasing church attendance, it should be added the "one-hour package" typically ties people into that congregation only at one point. For most adults it is the worship experience. For a few adults and most of the children it is the Sunday school. That is a "fail-disaster" system. If, for one reason or another, that one point of the relationship between that person and that congregation fails, the person may stop attending. If the adults are related to that congregation via corporate worship, a Men's Fellowship or the women's organization or an adult Sunday school class, participation in the choir and/or other points, the failure of that relationship at any one point is less likely to produce an inactive member. The frequency of worship attendance of adults who also are members of an adult class usually is higher than that of the parents who come for the "one-hour package."

A common response to the competing demands of the choir and the Sunday school is to schedule a fifteen- to thirty-minute fellowship period between the end of Sunday school and the beginning of worship.

4. Match Goals, Program Priorities, and Resources

Perhaps the most obvious means of using the power of program to increase attendance is in the value of matching goals and priorities in allocating resources. In dozens of congregations a persuasive argument can be made for the need to add a part-time staff person to call on persons with handicapping conditions. That, however, may do little to boost church attendance. Likewise building a youth choir of thirty-five voices often will do far more to increase worship attendance than allocating equivalent resources to developing a high school youth group.

If the primary goal is to increase the frequency of attendance of members, it may be appropriate to concentrate on expanding the adult Sunday school. If, however, the goal is to increase attendance by adding more members, it may be wise to place the top priority in the allocation of program resources to expanding the weekday program with preschool children and their parents or to focus on remarried couples. If the goal is to attract single males in their twenties, the appropriate program priority may be to strengthen the preaching.

The temptation in most congregations is to allocate resources in a manner designed to make the members happier or more comfortable. If the goal is to increase the attendance on Sunday morning, that often calls for a different allocation of resources ranging from staff time to use of the building to budgeting income to reserving the ten most desirable parking spaces for visitors rather than for the choir members.

Who makes the decisions in your congregation on (a) the goals in programming and (b) the allocation of scarce resources? Are those decisions designed to make members comfortable or to increase church attendance?

5. *Expand to a Full Music Program*

The overwhelming majority of church members appreciate the contribution a good vocal choir can make

to that Sunday morning
worship as the choir
leads the congregation in
praising God.

While this percentage
appears to shrink as the
size of the congregation
increases (it really goes
up), a broad generaliza-
tion is that the potential
number of members of
the adult choir is equivalent to approximately 10
to 12 percent of the
confirmed membership.

Expand your ministry of music!

Thus the three-hundred-member congregation has the
potential of a thirty- to thirty-five-voice adult choir. That
number maybe somewhat higher or lower depending on
(a) the time of rehearsal, (b) the choir director's ability
and persuasiveness in enlisting members, (c) the
organizing principles followed by the choir director, (d)
the performance standards enforced by the choir
director, (e) the age of the members (it usually is easier
to recruit people over forty for the choir than people
under thirty), and (f) other local variables.

In real life the one hundred-fifty-member congregation may have a choir of seven to fifteen people while the
thousand-member congregation may have a chancel
choir of only thirty-five to forty-five voices, rather than
close to a hundred.

Why? One reason is the chancel choir in the large
congregation often intimidates potential members who
believe they do not have *that* level of competence.

Frequently the choir director uses organizing principles designed to produce a choir of thirty-five to forty rather than large group principles. Sometimes the time of rehearsal is inconvenient for many potential choir members. In many large churches at least a fifth of the potential choir members either do not like the choir director and/or do not like the music chosen by that director.

What does this have to do with increasing church attendance? If your congregation includes more than five hundred members (and approximately one-third of all worshipers in a Protestant church on the typical Sunday in the United States are worshiping with a congregation of more than five hundred members), it may mean you should be thinking about a music program rather than simply counting the numbers of choirs. A reasonable quantifiable goal is to divide the number of members of your congregation by one hundred fifty. The resulting figure is the minimum number of music groups that will help lead worship on the typical Sunday morning.

Thus the twelve-hundred-member congregation might have a high school youth choir singing at the first service along with a handbell choir composed of mature adults. The second service might have a young adult choir singing the anthem while the more heavily attended third service (west of the Mississippi River that most heavily attended service may be the middle one) may include the chancel choir, a flute choir, and a brass ensemble on one Sunday morning while the next Sunday the music might be provided by the chancel choir, a women's handbell choir, and a children's choir. The music program at that twelve-hundred-member congregation also might include a drama group, a liturgical dance group, and a music encounter program for young children who discover the power of instrumental music as a means of expressing their creativity.

By contrast the 465-member congregation might have a youth choir at the first service and a children's choir and the chancel choir at the second service.

Six additional generalizations should be considered as you look at music as a means of increasing church attendance. First, an increase in the number of music groups in the worship experience usually will result in an increase in attendance. Second, it is legal for those who so choose to be active members of two or more music groups. Third, it often is unreasonable to expect any one choir director to relate effectively to children, youth, and adults, so it may be wise to rely on three or four different persons to organize and direct choirs rather than one. Fourth, a useful means of creating a second (or third) adult choir is to ask a different person to organize and direct it and schedule rehearsal at a different time. (In some large congregations one adult choir rehearses on Thursday evening and sings at eleven o'clock Sunday while another adult choir sings at an earlier service and rehearses at eleven.) Fifth, several large congregations regularly include three or four music groups in a sixty-minute service. It can be done. Finally, a music group often is the most attractive point of entry for many new members and usually is an exceptionally effective means of assimilating new-comers and causing them to feel wanted, needed, and appreciated. The ministry of music not only can make a magnificent contribution to the worship experience and to increasing attendance, it also should be perceived as an important component of any strategy for enlisting and assimilating new members.

With the exception of the all-male group, most vocal choirs are composed of a majority of women; one-fourth to one-third of the members are men. One means of both increasing church attendance and expanding male participation is to organize a men and boy's chorus and/or more instrumental groups. An instrumental group is more likely than a vocal group to be predominantly male.

Sometimes, however, those possibilities are thwarted because no one adequately appreciated the impact that real estate can have on music, worship, outreach, and church attendance.

5 REAL ESTATE CONSIDERATIONS DO INFLUENCE ATTENDANCE

For the life of me, I cannot understand why you folks asked to meet with us this evening," grumbled Harry Walker. "If you read the constitution and bylaws of our church, you can see the trustees are responsible for the property. We do not have any responsibility for program."

Harry was upset when three members of the evangelism committee had appeared, without invitation, at the April meeting of the Board of Trustees at Calvary Church. They had come to raise one question, "What are you trustees doing to expand the evangelistic outreach of this congregation?" Harry's response was, "That is none of our business. That's your responsibility, not ours!"

Harry was wrong. The actions, or inactions, of the trustees can have a powerful impact on the ability of a congregation to reach and serve people beyond the membership. Likewise, in many congregations those responsible for the real estate may have a tremendous impact on how many people appear for Sunday morning worship. This point can be illustrated by eleven examples. Tied for first place as the most important are five responsibilities usually assigned to the trustees.

1. Maintain a Clean and Attractive Building

The building should be clean, neat, and attractive from both the outside and inside. An attractive building

does attract people. An unattractive building repels. The responsibility for cleaning the building and keeping it clean should be clearly defined.

2. Use Lots of Signs

Both exterior and interior signs are important in helping first-time visitors find their way. The more densely populated the neighborhood and/or the larger the building and/or the more complicated the interior arrangement of the building, the more important are directional signs.

The beginning point is the signs along the roads and streets that direct motorists to your property. If off-street parking is available, "Park Here" signs can be useful as well as exterior signs that direct strangers to the proper door. One exterior sign should indicate in bold letters which parking places are reserved for visitors.

Interior signs should direct people to the office, the pastor's study, rest rooms, the fellowship hall, and classrooms. These should be attractive and easy-to-read signs placed at strategic points in the hallways.

3. The Nursery and Rest Rooms Are Important

The quality of the nursery is of great significance for any congregation seeking to reach mothers born since 1960. The inspection committee to identify the changes needed to modernize the nursery should include (a) three mothers with first-born children not yet one year old (they need not be members), (b) a doting grandfather who loves children and has influence with the trustees, and (c) one extremely militant and loving grandmother. Do *not* ask five men, all born before 1925, to constitute the inspection committee for the nursery!

The women's rest room can be a highly influential factor in (a) determining whether female first-time visitors will return, (b) influencing how long people will stay on Sunday morning, and (c) deciding whether or not to serve coffee during the fellowship period.

The inspection committee for the women's rest room should first visit the rest rooms in that new shopping mall to determine contemporary standards of quality before inspecting the women's rest room in your church. This committee obviously should be an all-female group if the goal is to meet contemporary expectations of modern women.

4. Offer Adequate Off-Street Parking

Once upon a time drivers were surprised and delighted to dis-cover a vacant and con-venient parking space at the end of their journey. Today many people place off-street parking in the same category of normal expectations as indoor plumbing and electric lights.

This is an especially critical issue for congregations that (a) are located west of Ohio (in the Northeast expectations in regard to off-street parking are lower than those west of Ohio), (b) expect to reach and serve people born after 1960, (c) plan to be in existence in the year 2003 (by which time most of those who now argue people will walk a quarter of a mile from where they park to get to church will be dead and forgotten), (d) expect to have mature women attending events during the week, and (e) plan to attract and keep a new generation of younger members through a full scale weekday and evening program schedule.

5. Provide Good Acoustics

As the proportion of churchgoers who have passed their sixtieth birthday continues to climb, the matter of

acoustics becomes more important. By 1995 this will be
a far more influential factor in determining who attends
worship on Sunday morning and where they attend than
it was in 1965 when many of the buildings with poor
acoustics already had been constructed.

6. *Provide Plenty of Space for Fellowship*

As life becomes more relational, the size, shape, and
quality of the place for fellowship becomes more
important.

Ideally, the room where the fellowship period will be
held *both* before *and* after worship will (a) be on the
same floor as the room used for corporate worship, (b)
be located between the main exit from the sanctuary
and the main exit from the building to the parking area,
(c) be able to accommodate comfortably all the people
who attend worship, (d) be designed so there can be *at
least* two places for people to be served refreshments,
one for adults and children and one for teenagers, and
(e) be designed with the cloakroom near the main
entrance and opposite the main entrance into the
sanctuary (the design should encourage people to stop
and talk before picking up their coats). This room also
should be furnished with several clusters of chairs for
those who prefer to sit while talking. (In general, people
who partake of refreshments while standing often stand
in the traffic lanes so the chairs and attractive displays
on the walls are necessary to offset this natural
tendency.)

This room also should have space on the walls for at
least four bulletin boards. One should be for news about

members and their joys and concerns. A second should contain congregational program notices. The third may carry denominational and general church news while the fourth should be a "conversation starter" bulletin board where strangers can gather and comment to one another on what they see posted there. If the fellowship period is outdoors on the patio, kiosks can replace or supplement the bulletin boards in the walls. Wise use of bulletin boards can convey to the first-time visitor this congregation is still alive.

7. Air Conditioning Can Make a Difference

Sooner or later the trustees of at least three-quarters of the church buildings in the United States will face the demand for central air conditioning. The simple rule of thumb is that if more than 75 percent of the new single family homes constructed in your county are built with central air conditioning, you probably should plan on air conditioning your church building. In most counties this is an essential part of a strategy to cancel the summer slump.

A common response is to fund most or all of the cost

of central air conditioning out of bequests. In a few churches, however, someone had the brilliant idea that it might be good to enable the people who will pay for it to enjoy the comfort of air conditioning before they die.

8. Can You Seat Too Many People?

Unquestionably the most difficult question facing the trustees in thousands of congregations concerns the seating arrangements in the nave. It appears that many houses of worship were constructed under one or more of the following operational assumptions:

a. Someday one of our members will be elected President of the United States, die while in office, the funeral service will be held here and so the nave must be sufficiently large to accommodate the crowd.[1]

b. The congregation consists largely of husband-wife couples with six to twelve children so the pews must be sufficiently long enough to accommodate the entire family in one pew.

c. The members are young, find it easy to climb stairs to worship on the second floor, and will never grow old.

d. All members and visitors will be slender and agile people who will experience no difficulty in climbing past people seated at the end of the pew in order to reach the vacant sections near the center of that pew.

---

[1] Between 1890 and 1906, 194,000 Protestant congregations in the United States added 6.3 million members for a total of 20.3 million members in 1906. They also increased the seating capacity of their sanctuaries from 41 million in 1890 to 55 million in 1906. That was a sign of a positive future orientation!

e. Sunday morning worship attendance will vary little from Sunday to Sunday or month to month, so it will not be necessary to adjust to the fact that attendance during Lent or on Christmas Eve may be double or triple the attendance in August.

f. None of our members will ever reach the age when a sloping floor makes it difficult to walk *down* to the chancel so the design can include a sloping floor to improve the view of the people seated in the rear pews. Or we will always serve Communion to people in the pews so the elderly will never have to walk down that sloping floor. (Also, young boys will never bring marbles to church on Sunday, and if they do, they will not drop them on that sloping floor.)

In at least a few congregations the passage of time has made one or two of these assumptions obsolete.

Three useful experiences for those responsible for remodeling the nave to accommodate contemporary reality could be to:

a. Stand outside the church on Sunday morning and count how many worshipers (1) come alone, (2) come as part of a two-person group, (3) come as part of a three-person group, and (4) come as part of a group including four or more persons.

b. Visit two recently constructed airport terminals and study the seating arrangements.

c. At one minute before the beginning of worship on a typical Sunday morning count the number of worshipers seated at the end of a pew and count the number of worshipers seated in the interior section of the pews.

These three sources of data may enable the trustees

to discover the seating arrangements that people prefer.

Ideally, the place of worship will be designed with chairs, rather than pews, so the number of chairs each week will be the number of people expected for worship minus 2 or 3 percent. Thus on most Sundays the obvious conclusion will be, "The crowd was so large we had to bring in more chairs."

In addition, the chairs can be arranged to give people more space on either side and also to increase the number of seats on the aisles.

If, however, the nave has pews attached to the floor (movable pews now exist and can be purchased as replacements) and if the seating capacity greatly exceeds the attendance on the typical Sunday, it may be wise to remove some of the pews at the rear and/or in front in order to make it appear "our church is full" on the typical Sunday.

This is a very significant issue in those congregations (a) in which the attendance rarely exceeds 60 percent of the available seating, (b) that are considering a change to two worship experiences on Sunday morning, but the proposal is rejected because of the excessive number of pews in the nave, and (c) that average more than seventy to eighty-five at Sunday morning worship (in smaller congregations those present count the faces and note the absence of familiar faces; in larger congregations people tend to count the furniture and note the number of vacant pews).

In simple terms, the worship committee or the church growth committee of today, not the building committee of several decades ago, should control the seating arrangements for worship if the goal is to increase attendance!

9. Do You Need to Remodel?

Those congregations meeting in a building constructed before 1960 may conclude that the goal of any significant increase in worship attendance cannot be achieved unless the building is remodeled.

In many cases this will require expanding the space for worship; in others it may mean remodeling the sanctuary (perhaps enlarging the chancel as some front pews are removed) to reduce the seating arrangements; in more than a few the remodeling will bring the classrooms, rest rooms, nursery, and corridors up to contemporary standards; while in some the major focus will be on making the building more attractive and accessible to strangers.

Back in the 1950s it was widely assumed that "architectural evangelism" would work; if a congregation constructed an attractive new building, it would soon be filled. Experience has demonstrated that was a naive expectation and now it is widely recognized that while a new building may not attract people, an unattractive or functionally obsolete structure often does repel people.

10. Has the Time Come to Rebuild?

Perhaps 2 to 3 percent of all American Protestant congregations have the mixed blessing of an obsolete

building on a desirable
parcel of land of ade-
quate size at a prize
location. For them the
most effective path to
increasing worship at-
tendance may be to raze
that obsolete structure
and replace it with a
more attractive and
functional meeting
place. If it needs to be
done, why not go ahead
and do it now rather than
pass the buck to another
generation?

11. Is Your Location Obsolete?

At least 10 percent of all Protestant congregations
are meeting at a site and/or in a building where the best
long-range solution is to relocate. In a fair number of
cases this was a poor location from day one—often
because the land was a gift. In others the congregation
has outgrown both the building and the parcel of land.
(As a general rule, a congregation averaging one
hundred at worship and expecting to be in existence at
that location in the year 2010 should have two acres of
land. For each increase of one hundred in worship
attendance add one acre, thus the congregation
averaging four hundred at worship needs a minimum of

five acres of land. A Christian Day School will require a larger parcel of land for the same sized congregation.)

In the majority of cases both the location and the size of the parcel of land were adequate when that first building was constructed. The passage of time, however, has turned what once was a good location into an inadequate or obsolete location today.

One of the big differences between the middle and upper class Anglo congregations of today and most Jewish, Asian, Black, and working class Anglo congregations is the former often are barred by feelings of guilt from relocating the meeting place while the latter often relocate with far less guilt and more satisfaction.

This suggestion of possible relocation, of course, is irrelevant to those congregations that expect to dissolve within a decade or those that plan to change from a primary emphasis on worship, nurture, and evangelism to the role of a landlord housing a variety of community agencies and their programs.

Do your trustees see themselves as highly influential leaders in determining whether or not the worship attendance in your church will increase or decrease? If the answer is that they do not perceive themselves in that role, it may be the time has come to create ad hoc action committees, but that is another subject for the last chapter.

6 INSTITUTIONAL FACTORS

A variety of factors influence both the people's choice to become part of a worshiping community and the frequency of their participation. Many of these are factors today's leaders of a particular congregation have a substantial degree of control over; others are under the control of the individual. Forty of the ones over which the leaders have varying degrees of control have been described in previous chapters. Four remain that can be grouped under the general umbrella of institutional considerations. History, societal trends, denominational traditions and rules, congregational values, and the decisions of preceding generations of leaders often have a profound influence on these four approaches to increasing church attendance. It probably will be far more difficult for today's leaders to implement these four suggestions. All four should be perceived as part of a long-term strategy, not as ideas that can be implemented overnight.

1. Become a High Expectation Congregation

From a long-term perspective the most influential single approach to increasing church attendance is to raise the level of expectations. All of us respond, in varying degrees, to the expectations others place on us. The New Testament makes it clear that Jesus projected extremely high expectations on all who would choose to follow him. The Christian faith is a high demand religion.

A century ago both Protestant and Roman Catholic

THIS IS KNOWN AS LIVING HIGH OFF THE HOPES OF OTHERS!

HIGHER DEMANDS

LONGER HOURS

What do we expect of our people?

—FRIAR TUCK.

churches in America placed relatively high expectations on their members. During the first six or seven decades of this century many denominations and congregations lowered the expectations placed on seminarians, ministers, members, and leaders. In recent years it appears a reversal of that trend has begun. In some congregations the rule still applies that a member must be absent from Sunday morning worship for more than one hundred consecutive Sundays before his or her name can be removed from the membership rolls involuntarily. Increasingly common, however, are the churches that require regular attendance of anyone seeking to become a member.

A simple example of the impact of high expectations can be seen in those congregations that require all persons seeking to become members (including those seeking to transfer their membership from another congregation of that same denomination) to participate in a twenty- or thirty-five- or forty-five-week membership class before joining. In some a person may join at that individual's choice after sixteen or twenty weeks, but everyone is expected to attend every session for the entire seven or eight or nine or ten months. The frequency of attendance of the new members of these churches usually is far higher than in the congregations that require prospective new members to attend only one or two or three sessions of an orientation class.

The same pattern can be seen in those congregations that expect every member to be a tither. The frequency of attendance at worship usually is far higher than in those congregations where the majority of members contribute less than 2 percent of their annual income to that church. In many congregations there is a consistent correlation between the level of financial contributions of a member and that member's frequency of attendance at corporate worship.

To move in the direction of becoming a high expectation church may be a difficult and controversial decision in those congregations that now resemble a voluntary organization. It may mean running counter to the culture of that denomination. It may alienate those who joined convinced this was a voluntary association where the extent of participation was determined by the member, not by the institution. It cannot be accomplished overnight, but it can be the most effective single approach to increasing the frequency of church attendance by the members. The evidence suggests it also may be an effective means of attracting a large number of new members, but that also usually requires excellent preaching, a meaningful worship experience, and a high quality ministry of Christian education.

2. Examine the Community Image and Name

"Bethany Community Church?" mused the sixty-five-year-old resident of this city of 200,000 residents. "I'm afraid you've got me on that one. I've lived here most of my life, but I can't place any Bethany Church. Maybe if you could tell me the name of the minister, I could help you."

"The pastor is named Ben Harrison," answered the stranger.

"Oh, Dr. Harrison's church!" exclaimed the old-timer. "Why didn't you tell me you were looking for Dr. Harrison? Everybody here knows good old Doc Harrison. He's one of the finest men you'll ever meet anywhere. If you go west of here on this highway for about a mile, make a left at the stop light in front of the high school, go about two miles on that street, that's Wayland Avenue, you'll see Dr. Harrison's church on your right. It's a dark red brick building. You can't miss it!"

That conversation, which is replicated many times every week all across the nation, illustrates the second of these four institutional factors that should be taken into account by anyone seeking to increase the size of the crowd on Sunday morning.

For many congregations the dominant facet of their identity in the larger community is in the personality and/or tenure of the pastor. Dr. Benjamin Harrison, who founded Bethany Community Church in 1953, is a widely known figure in that city even though his nondenominational congregation averages fewer than 140 people at worship on Sunday. Many years ago he served on the school board for two terms, he was president of the Kiwanis Club, and seven years ago he headed the United Appeal drive. Currently he is on the city council, appears regularly on television, and every year he sends at least three or four dozen letters to the editor of the morning newspaper. Everyone, or so it seems, knows Dr. Harrison. He is a very articulate, witty, extroverted, liberal, well-educated, and energetic community leader. Hardly anyone, however, knows anything about his congregation.

At the other extreme is the large Protestant congregation that worships in a magnificent building located on a major traffic artery and includes a large proportion of community leaders in the membership. The twenty-two-year pastorate of a famous minister came to an inglorious end in 1976 when he left town, church, and family to live in California with an attractive woman from the choir twenty years his junior. He was followed by a three-year healing ministry by a gracious, loving, and nearly anonymous pastor in his early sixties who was followed by the seven-year pastorate of a colorless and nearly invisible nonentity. The current minister, the Reverend Mr. Whatishisname, is known to more than one-half of the members and perhaps thirteen or fourteen nonmembers. Today his congregation's community image is largely in the prestigious membership and in the past which people refuse to forget.

Other congregations in this city in which the community image largely reflects the membership include a large working class church on the east side, two different congregations that carry the word "university" in their names, a prestigious Black Baptist congregation, a twelve-year-old vigorous Korean church, the Episcopal cathedral, and the First Presbyterian Church which includes a larger number of today's "shakers and movers" than any other church in town.

Several churches are best known by specific programs and ministries. These include the First Baptist Church which fills the sanctuary five times in mid-December as people come to see and hear the "living Christmas tree" that consists of a 110-voice choir arranged on six levels in the shape of a Christmas tree complete with pine boughs, a nondenominational church that includes nearly a thousand people in the Sunday school, a nearby downtown congregation that feeds an average of one hundred people daily every day of the year in its soup kitchen, a 200-member congregation that sends four medical teams to Central America every year, and a congregation that operates the most demanding Christian Day School of any church in the state.

A fourth facet of community image is reflected in two congregations who boast their buildings are now in the historic register, a congregation with its building in the middle of a two-acre, park-like site across the street from the state capitol and a newer congregation that meets in a huge building on the north edge of the city in a structure that appears at first glance to be the product of mating a space shuttle with a pumpkin. In each case the dominant characteristic of the community identity is the property.

Instead of building their community image around the Good News, a small proportion of churches have found their image is derived from bad news. In one case it is a congregation that has split twice in a quarter of a century with the dissidents angrily walking out to form new congregations. In another the treasurer was convicted in the civil courts for embezzling money. In a third two successive ministers were discharged on the grounds of immorality and were forced to surrender their ordination credentials. In each of these congregations the task of rebuilding people's trust overshadowed all other priorities and that included creating a more positive community image.

Finally, for many congregations their distinctive community image is largely a reflection of their denominational affiliation. Back in the 1950s this often was a net asset since such words as "Methodist" or "Presbyterian" in the name of a congregation automatically attracted many people who were loyal to that denominational family. In recent decades, however, the erosion of denominational loyalties, especially west of the Rocky Mountains, has greatly reduced the value of the denominational affiliation as the primary component in the community image of a congregation. Anyone who looks at the names of congregations established since 1965 will see that many people have concluded that words such as "Lutheran," "Reformed," "Mennonite," "Brethren," "Church of Christ," "Assemblies of God," and "Baptist" (especially in the North) can best be omitted from the name of that new congregation.

What is the image nonmembers have of your congregation? Is that community image based primarily on the pastor? Or the members? Or the property? Or the program? Or some widely publicized scandal? Or the denominational affiliation? What do you want it to be? Can you change it? How?

The winner, of course, is the congregation that outsiders see (a) is led by a committed Christian minister who is a loving, gregarious, and energetic personality who also is an articulate and attractive preacher and excels at conducting funerals, (b) is composed of members who act out of the two great commandments that Jesus told us about, (c) offers a rich variety of high quality programs designed to meet the needs of today's people in today's world, and (d) places a high priority on missions and outreach. Inasmuch as only one in ten thousand congregations meets all four of those criteria, the competition is not as tough as it may first appear.

For several decades the most widely used word to name a new congregation in American Protestantism was "First." In several denominations the second congregation from that denominational family to be established in that community was named "Second Church" and the third carried that word as the first part of its name.

In recent years it appears the most widely used word in naming a new Protestant congregation is "Community." Ironically this trend, which began to become widespread in the 1930s, was overshadowed in the 1960s by the decline in the concept of a geographical parish.

This question comes up not only in naming new congregations, but also may arise following (a) the relocation of the meeting place, (b) a merger with another congregation or, in some cases, (c) a denominational merger which means two congregations with the same name are now in the same denomination.

Ideally the name will be short, easy to spell, simple to pronounce, attractive, and appealing. The name should not carry any negative connotations. It should not be a name that may be confused with the name of another congregation nearby. In several denominations the tradition has been to name congregations after biblical figures, places, or concepts (St. John, Bethel, or Trinity). In others the custom has been to identify the congregation with its location in the name (Main Street, Lake Avenue, North Side).

That is a value on which there is less than complete agreement. It can be useful, however, to pick a name that can be translated into a logogram and that logo can be used to reinforce the community identity. Trinity, Good Shepherd, St. Mark, Church of the Cross, and Pilgrim are examples.

The big debate today is over whether or not the denominational affiliation should be included in the name, on the bulletin board in front of the building, in the newspaper advertisement, and on the letterhead of the church's stationery. This clearly is a delicate subject that has largely ideological arguments on one side and pragmatic considerations on the other. One side declares a jackass is the only creature to deny its heritage and any definition of the interdependent character of congregations demands the denominational affiliation be part of the name. The other side argues that words such as "Baptist" or "Lutheran" or "Reformed" are widely perceived as exclusionary words and the name should convey an image of openness and suggest outsiders are welcome. That is one of the arguments for the use of "Community" or simply a place name or for a nondenominational label such as "Christ Church" or "Calvary Chapel." People on this side also argue that "United Church of Christ" conveys a misleading image in the Southwest where it may be confused with the Church of Christ or that "Methodist" or "Presbyterian" now repel rather than attract people.

Part of the argument that certain words that once attracted now repel is based on the fact that in the early 1980s the Methodists gained only six new members from other churches for every ten lost to other denominations, while in the 1950s they gained fifteen for every ten who left for another church. Presbyterians now gain eight from other churches for every ten who leave compared to a fourteen-to-ten ratio in the 1950s. This does not prove the name is the critical factor since many other causes could be cited for that change in the affiliation/disaffiliation ratio. The change in that ratio does suggest, however, that the denominational labels do not have the drawing power they once displayed.

Several pastors insist the best name is "Advent Church" since that places the congregation at or near the top in the listings in the Yellow Pages.

How do you use the name of your congregation to make it easier for potential visitors to identify who you are?

3. *Yoked or Separate?*

Far more important than the name for tens of thousands of congregations is the fact they share a pastor with another congregation or two or three and this, more than any other factor, determines their schedule, shapes their image, and influences their program. Approximately one-half of the nearly 38,000 United Methodist congregations are in circuits consisting of two or more churches served by one minister. That custom still prevails, to a lesser degree, in several other denominations.

The evidence appears to be heavily on the side of the

argument that contends that if numerical growth is a factor or if the morale of the minister is considered to be important, it may be better to find a minister with part-time or full-time secular employment rather than to share a pastor with one or more congregations.[1]

The traditional argument has been (a) a minister should be engaged in only the practice of ministry and no other income-producing vocation and (b) inasmuch as thousands of congregations are too small to justify or afford a full-time resident pastor, therefore the only feasible alternative is to have one minister serve two or more congregations in order "to make a salary."

When the growth pattern of congregations served by a part-time minister with secular employment is compared with growth pattern of churches that share a minister with another congregation, the results suggest that if the primary goal is to increase the size of the crowd on Sunday morning, it may be better to choose the part-time minister with secular employment. The number of seminary graduates interested in this possibility has increased sharply in recent years so this

---

[1]An introduction to this concept, based on the CODE prospect in New York state can be found in John Y. Elliott, *Our Pastor Has an Outside Job* (Valley Forge, Pa.: Judson Press, 1980).

is now more attractive than it was several years ago. In the late 1980s The United Methodist Church had the largest number of congregations of any denomination that shared a minister with one or more other churches. At the other end of the spectrum was the Southern Baptist Convention which included the largest number of "bivocational ministers" who served only one congregation while also carrying a full-time secular job.

It must be added that in some denominations and in many congregations other values and goals take precedence over numerical growth and for those churches this may not be an attractive alternative for increasing church attendance. Perhaps the most widespread objection in this arrangement often means the minister ceases to be economically dependent on the congregation and/or the denomination.

Breaking the yoke and finding the right match between minister and congregation has turned out to be a very effective means of increasing church attendance in scores, perhaps hundreds of congregations. The pastor now is available for all of Sunday morning and can concentrate his or her energies on expanding the program and outreach of that congregation which cannot help but increase attendance.

4. Create Places for Men

One of the rarely discussed and largely overlooked developments of the 1920–1955 era in American Protestantism was the increased capability of Protestant congregations to attract adult males, and especially working class men, to Sunday morning worship. While the historical evidence is somewhat scanty, it appears that in the 1920s men accounted for approximately 40 percent or less of the adults in attendance at Sunday morning worship in the typical Protestant congregation and relatively few working class males attended church in the 1920s.

For several years, polls by the Gallup organization have reported that women, by a 56-to-44 margin, are more likely than men to say they attended worship during the past week and to declare that religion is important in their lives. Among those who respond that religion is *not* important in their lives, men outnumber women 63-to-37. In contrast, in 1952 Gallup reported that among those Americans who said they attended worship at least twice a month, women outnumbered men by a lesser (53-to-47) ratio.

By 1985 the ratio in several old-line denominations had changed to approximately 60 or 61 or 62 percent female and 40 or 39 or 38 percent male on the typical Sunday morning. This trend toward a substantial female majority was most apparent in the United Church of Christ, the Presbyterian Church (USA), The United Methodist Church, the Unitarian-Universalist Association, the Christian Church (Disciples of Christ), and in thousands of Black churches.

Is this a permanent return to the patterns of the early 1920s? Or can it be changed? The experiences of those congregations that have seen an increase in the number of men present for Sunday morning worship suggests this can be a productive route for those interested in increasing church attendance.

Among the most common characteristics of congregations that report an increase in male attendance these four stand out repeatedly.

First, the identification of adult males with that

congregation is reinforced by a series of redundant ties. These may include a large number of men teaching in the Sunday church school, being in an all-male music group, video taping and editing the tape from the Sunday morning worship service for use in a local TV station, participating in the predominantly male or all-male mission work camp trip, serving on ad hoc action committees (men tend to be less interested in participating in standing committees), sharing in the annual bazaar or mission fair sponsored by the women's organization, belonging to the "Grandfathers' Club," which is a support group and lobby for the weekday preschool, assisting in the Sunday morning worship experience, all-male Bible study groups and/or all-male adult Sunday school classes, a Men's Fellowship, the six-man brass ensemble, serving breakfast before the first worship service on Sunday morning, delivering the Sunday morning children's sermon or working on a variety of projects through which they can express their creativity through their hands.

Second, the preaching is specific, not abstract, filled with visual imagery and speaks to the concerns of today's adult males.

Third, the experiences of these churches suggest

two types of staff persons who tend to elicit male involvement. One is the male pastor who entered the ordained ministry as a second career following several years in a secular vocation (relating to other men). Some search committees have reservations about the candidate who prepared for the ministry after working a decade in a factory or in construction or in business, but such experience can be an asset to the congregation that seeks to involve males.

The other especially effective staff person is a woman, especially the ordained female minister. In contrast with male staff persons, who presume automatic relationships with other men, women recognize that they live in a male-dominated world and consequently often make a conscious effort to relate to (and "get along with") men. Ordained women often appear more willing to accept and fulfill the authority that goes with the office of pastor, and many males appreciate that. When seeking a new staff member, lay or ordained, you may want to consider a woman, especially one for whom the parish ministry is a second career.

Finally, and clearly most influential, these congregations display a conscious, consistent, persistent, determined, redundant, and comprehensive effort to increase the participation of adult males. The leaders are not content to sit back, wring their hands, and declare, "I wish the men would be as faithful in their attendance as the women are."

As you reflect on the impact of these four institutional forces on church attendance, is there an obvious beginning point for your congregation? Do you want to move toward becoming a high expectation church? Or is the best place to begin an effort to strengthen the community identity of your congregation? How can you make the image you convey to outsiders more attractive? Does the name communicate exclusionary or attractive images? If your congregation shares a minister with another congregation, do you see that as a positive or a negative influence on church attendance? What is the proportion of adults on Sunday morning who are male? If it is below 47 percent, can that percentage be increased? How?

As you respond to these and other questions, you may now be ready to ask, What do we do next?

7 WHAT NEXT?

Having read this far and perhaps already well into the process of sorting out which of these forty-four suggestions for increasing attendance fit your congregation, you also may be asking, What do we do next?

One alternative, and certainly the one requiring the least initiative and no creativity, is to do nothing.

A second is to wish that someone else would pick up at least one or two of these suggestions and begin the process of implementation. That means, however, surrendering the initiative. Whenever we shift expectations from ourselves to someone else, we give up the opportunity of functioning in an initiating role and move into the role of reacting to the leadership of others. When we choose that course of action, we are asking others to shape our future and we will react to their initiative.

Perhaps the most distinctive characteristic of passive organizations is the large number of members who "wish someone would do something." They are surrendering control to the tiny number (often zero) of members who are willing to accept and fulfill the role of initiating leader or, more often, are waiting for external forces to determine their future.

A third course of action might be to select two or three of these suggestions and bring them to the attention of the governing board of your congregation. This may produce one of four results.

Ideally the governing board will accept your recommendations and take the action necessary to implement them. More likely this will simply add to what is an already overloaded agenda and your suggestions will be shelved until the governing board has more discretionary time to allot to minor issues.

Or, you may be listened to with real interest and genuine respect, but the minutes will reveal ". . . and a very interesting report on alternatives for improving our worship attendance was presented by (write in your name)." Often that will be the end of that.

Or, and this may be the most tempting alternative in congregations with a network of standing committees, your suggestions will be referred for further consideration to the appropriate standing committee.

That introduces the fourth course of action you might choose after completing this book. It may strike you as the logical next step to take your suggestions directly

to the appropriate
standing committees
such as worship or nur-
ture or care of members
or evangelism or con-
gregational life.

On the face of it that
may appear to be the
most attractive next
step. In fact there are
only five things wrong
with that alternative.

First, standing commit-
tees typically prefer the
status quo and naturally
tend to perpetuate continuity rather than to introduce
changes. Most of the forty-four suggestions in this book
represent discontinuity and are a challenge to the status quo.

Second, only rarely do standing committees respond
favorably to ideas that did not originate within that
group. You may be a victim of the N.I.H. syndrome.
(N.I.H. means Not Invented Here.)

Third, many of the suggestions offered here go
beyond the jurisdiction of any one person or committee.
Standing committees usually are reluctant to take action
on any issue unless it is clearly and completely within
their jurisdiction. (Standing committees usually operate
on the assumption that everything is prohibited unless
clearly and unquestionably permitted.)

Fourth, many of these forty-four suggestions for
increasing attendance require a long time frame in order
to adapt them to the unique personality of your
congregation, and most standing committees function in

a shorter time frame. Finally, standing committees naturally will make their own central responsibility (music, missions, Christian education, property, finance, social action) the top priority in their discussions. It is a rare congregation that has a standing committee concerned primarily with the size of the crowd on Sunday morning. That may mean that your suggestions will not receive the favorable attention you seek if you take them directly to what appears to be the appropriate standing committee.

That brief introduction into the nature of standing committees may lead you to consider a fifth alternative. This would be to seek to become a member of the appropriate standing committee that is concerned with worship attendance and, after you have become a member, to introduce your suggestions as an insider. This potential next step has considerable merit and also gives you time to tailor your suggestions to the unique personality of your congregation and to the priorities of that standing committee. For some people in certain congregations this may be the most productive course of action. Usually it requires considerable patience, persistence, and an understanding that most good ideas are rejected the first time they are presented. Thus this alternative often requires huge quantities of persistence and the capability to keep pushing what you are convinced are good ideas.

Those who do not display that amount of persistence and patience may be attracted to a sixth possibility. This is to ask for the creation of an ad hoc action committee that is directed to increase the average attendance at Sunday morning worship by 15 percent within a year. Ideally this ad hoc group also will be granted the authority to take such actions as are necessary in order to reach that goal. If that

is not possible, an acceptable compromise could be to give this ad hoc group power to implement changes unless these proposed changes are vetoed by the governing board within forty-five days after they are first presented to that board. (Typically it is easier to secure the withholding of a veto from a governing board than it is to secure that board's approval of a proposed course of action. Furthermore, the temptation to amend is far greater when the board is asked to approve a proposed course of action than when the issue is simply the withholding of a veto.)

Among the many reasons this course of action should be given serious consideration are the basic characteristics of the typical ad hoc action committee. Perhaps the two central characteristics that set them apart from the typical standing committee are (a) the standing committee often hesitates to tread on someone else's turf or meddle in the jurisdiction of another board while the normal ad hoc committee assumes everything is permitted unless specifically and clearly prohibited and (b) a standing committee on Christian education or evangelism or missions or other functional concerns can never complete that task. They continue to meet regularly for decades while the ad hoc action committee has a deadline after which it can cease to function. Thus when the special committee that was created to construct a building completes that task, it normally dissolves. When the special committee appointed to plan and conduct the celebration of the fiftieth anniversary of the founding of the congregation fulfills that responsibility, it adjourns.

Ad hoc action committees have the motivation of not being able to disband until the task is fulfilled.

Thus if a special ad hoc committee is created to increase worship attendance by 15 percent within a year, it will tend to place a greater emphasis on reaching that goal within a year than on not stepping on the toes of another committee. The deadline requires the assignment must be quantified. The ad hoc action committee can be held accountable and the pressure is to accomplish now rather than to postpone until a more favorable time.

The special ad hoc action committee also tends to (a) be goal-oriented rather than concerned with the preservation of the status quo, (b) be open to new ideas and to encourage creativity, (c) have permission to mobilize resources, (d) place a higher value on results rather than on tradition in evaluating alternative courses of action, (e) attract activists, doers, optimists and change-oriented individuals, and (f) meet deadlines and fulfill goals.

If none of these alternatives appeals to you, a seventh possible course of action remains for the individual who concludes, "I'm the only one in our congregation who displays any interest in enlarging the size of the crowd on Sunday morning. The governing body already has more than it can do; our standing committees are concerned only with property, Christian education, missions, and finances; and I don't know of anyone who would be interested in serving on a special ad hoc action committee to increase church attendance. What can I do?"

The answer is to change the focus from increasing worship attendance to a strategy for planned change from within an organization. This normally requires following these four steps in this sequence.

First is the necessity of encouraging others to catch your feelings of discontent. As long as people are happy with the status quo, they will not seek to change it. Therefore your first step must be to arouse more discontent over what you perceive to be a low level of worship attendance. This might be done by emphasizing the low worship attendance-to-membership ratio or by comparing the attendance with a similar type congregation with the same number of members but a higher level of attendance or by comparisons with the past.

After you have enlisted two or three or four allies who now also believe church attendance can and should be increased, you move to the second step which is to create an initiating group. This small group must be convinced something can be done to improve the level of attendance. This is the group that proposes a specific course of action. Thus this group might propose the creation of the ad hoc action committee suggested earlier.

The third and essential step before seeking to

"Wherever two or three
are gathered
there is always
the possibility of change!"
— FRIAR TUCK

implement a particular plan is to broaden your base of support. This may include securing the active approval of several influential leaders and the neutrality of one or two individuals who have the power to veto your plans. This mobilization of support also may include votes, money, people's time and, perhaps most difficult of all, commitment to a brighter future.

After you have broadened your support base, you may conclude it would be wise to work through the proposed action plan with this expanded support group. While some initiating leaders may find this difficult to believe, it often happens that the plans of the original initiating group are not only revised, but also they can be greatly improved in this third stage.

Finally, in the fourth step you seek formal approval or adoption and implementation of your action plan. This step should not be taken until after a full support group has been mobilized. The three keys in this process of planned change from within an organization to keep in mind at this stage are (a) if your plans include what is perceived as a radical change, you may want to compromise by suggesting, "Let's try it for only a year and see what happens" (it often is easier to secure approval of a temporary system than of a permanent change and the year allows the opponents time to talk themselves into supporting the change), (b) if your proposal is rejected you should perceive this as the normal and predictable response to a new idea and ask yourself, "When do you think would be the best time to reintroduce this idea and are there any changes in it that should be made before we introduce it again?" and (c) if your congregation resembles a voluntary association of people more than it does a covenant community, you should not bring your proposal to a vote until you are reasonably sure it will be approved.[1]

Which of these alternatives appears to be the logical next step for you as you seek to increase church attendance in your congregation?

---

[1]For additional detail on the process of planned change from within an organization see Lyle E. Schaller, *The Change Agent* (Nashville: Abingdon Press, 1972), pp. 78-118, or Donald L. Kirkpatrick, *How to Manage Change Effectively* (San Francisco: Jossey-Bass, Publishers, 1985), pp. 76-150, or Lyle E. Schaller, *Getting Things Done* (Nashville: Abingdon Press, 1986), chapter 6.